2008

TWENTY20 VISION

TWENTY20 VISION

My Life and Inspiration

MUSHTAQ AHMED

with Andy Sibson

Methuen

First published in Great Britain 2006 by
Methuen Publishing Ltd
11–12 Buckingham Gate
London
SW1E 6LB

10 9 8 7 6 5 4 3 2 1

A CIP catalogue record for this book is available from the British Library.

ISBN-10: 0413 776255
ISBN-13: 9780413776259

Printed and bound in Great Britain by MPG Books, Bodmin, Cornwall

Thank you

I have to thank my parents and family for providing the love and guidance that has supported me throughout my life.

My wife, Uzma Mushtaq, has given me the strength to continue at times when I have faltered. I thank her with all my heart.

Gary Mellor, my friend and agent, helped to create the circumstances for my renewed success in England. Thank you, Gary.

Roger Myall put me in touch with Andy Sibson, who knew what I was trying to say and helped me to say it. I thank both men for their efforts on my behalf. Thanks also to Darren Long for providing some early notes to assist with the development of this book.

Zulqarnain helped me find my way back to the Creator and I thank both each day.

Contents

List of Illustrations

Acknowledgements

The publisher wishes to thank the following for permission to reproduce photographs: Patrick Eagar, Roger Ockenden and the *Nottingham Evening Post*/Dominic Lepinski. Other photographs from private collections. The publisher has made every effort to trace copyright holders and seek permission. We apologise for any unintended omissions and would be pleased to receive information that would enable us to rectify any inaccuracies.

Statistics and records sourced from *Wisden Cricketers' Almanack* by kind permission of John Wisden & Co Ltd.

Foreword by Imran Khan

I was delighted when Mushtaq Ahmed invited me to write the foreword to his autobiography. I had the great fortune to be captaining the Pakistan side when he first burst on the scene. You must remember that in the late 1980s the leg-spinner had almost disappeared from the game of cricket at its highest levels. Pakistan, and indeed the whole cricket world, were lucky to have Abdul Qadir and then Mushy to fly the flag for this most recondite of skills. They kept the flame burning and ensured one of cricket's most delicate and elusive arts was not lost.

Reading Mushy's account of his early life, there was so much that struck home with me. I too experienced the hard school of playing with men and older boys much better than me, desperately hoping for a bat or a bowl. I have to admit that my privileged background made it much easier for me, but the determination Mushy and his friend Waqar showed in improving their cricket against all odds is an example to all, and the patience and perseverance they learnt was a crucial element of their success in the Test arena. I believe that in cricket, as in politics, you cannot really achieve great success until you have been through the mill and learnt the hard way.

In this book, it is instructive to see again an account of the poor structure and organisation of Pakistan cricket. Any autobiography from a Pakistan player of this period can be read as a devastating indictment of our system. Pakistan has enjoyed an amazing wealth of talent over the past twenty years: spinners such as Saqlain and Mushy himself, bowlers like Waqar and Wasim, and now Shoaib, and a golden age of batting from Salim Malik to Saeed Anwar and Inzamam; it is frustrating that performances remain inconsistent.

Not many books can boast the level of detail this possesses on the nature of leg-spin and the tactics employed to dismiss batsman.

What underlies the whole is Mushtaq's own natural attacking instincts, and these were what really made him stand out and what compelled me as captain to stick by him in the face of opposition from selectors and even team-mates. The fact he was an adventurous player made me insist on his selection for the World Cup of 1992. You will see from his stories that Mushtaq, for one, is a cricketer who is never afraid to lose, and as such he has the potential to win games for you from apparently hopeless positions.

Midway through the 1992 World Cup we were 50-1 outsiders. Our final victory was an incredible comeback, and, as you will read, meant so much for the people of Pakistan. Conventional wisdom has it that bowlers should use defensive tactics in one-day cricket. I used Mushtaq, as well as Wasim and Aaqib Javed, to attack, and let them know I did not care how many runs they conceded. Mushtaq's googly to dismiss Graeme Hick in the final is one of the great moments in modern Pakistan cricket.

The issue of ball-tampering is never far from the headlines. Now that everyone is using reverse swing (it was central to England's Ashes victory in 2005) it is easy to forget how controversial it once was. In *Twenty20 Vision* you can read the inside story of the skill Wasim and Waqar applied to the craft of reverse swing at a time when this technique was little understood, especially by the English press. These magnificent craftsmen had to put up with a tide of innuendo – here Mushtaq sets the record straight.

I am delighted too that Mushtaq is enjoying such success with my old county, Sussex. Under John Barclay we had come so close in 1981, and it seemed destined that the historic club was never to win the Championship pennant. Taking a hundred wickets in a season is a rare achievement indeed, and Mushtaq's success in 2003 was central to the long-awaited Championship victory. Mushtaq has a wonderful record in county cricket, and his popularity at Hove, and indeed around the country, is well deserved. Not many overseas players have been as consistent and successful.

Very few sports books are as revealing, candid and perceptive as *Twenty20 Vision*. I hope you have as much enjoyment reading it as Mushtaq himself did writing it. However, all of us, and especially

Sussex fans, hope there is plenty more to come from Mushtaq
Ahmed the cricketer, and that this excellent book does not bring
down the curtain on a wonderful career.

Chronology

Mushtaq Ahmed Chronology
Compiled by Andy Sibson

Born Sahiwal, Pakistan 28 June 1970

1985   Makes debut for Multan U19s at the age of fifteen.

1986/87   Scores 75 runs on his debut for Multan against Hyderabad. Selected for Punjabi Chief Minister's XI against England taking 6-85 in 36 overs. Debuts for United Bank in the Patron's Trophy. Leading wicket-taker in the Youth World Cup in Australia.

1988/89   Makes ODI debut for Pakistan in Sharjah against Sri Lanka. Don Kuruppu becomes his first international wicket. His debut figures are: 9.3 overs, 1 maiden 2 wickets for 33 runs.

1989/90   Tours India and Australia and plays in the Australasia Cup in Sharjah. Makes Test debut in Adelaide. His first Test wicket is Mark Taylor.

1990/91   Plays ODIs in Pakistan against New Zealand and West Indies. Selected for the Test team against West Indies.

1991/92   Helps Pakistan to become World Cup winners in Australia. Joint-second leading wicket-taker with sixteen tournament wickets. Tours England.

1992/93   Tours West Indies, New Zealand, Australia, South Africa and Zimbabwe.

1993   Plays for Somerset in the English County Championship, taking 85 wickets and scoring almost 500 runs. Leading wicket-taker in England.

1993/94   Tours New Zealand and Sri Lanka.

1995   Finishes the English County Championship season for Somerset with 95 wickets, behind only Anil Kumble in the standings.
Scores 20 in the highest last-wicket partnership (57 with Inzamam-ul-Haq) for Pakistan to beat Australia in Karachi.

1995/96   First Test 'five-for' in the first innings of the Second Test against Australia in Hobart. First 10-wicket Test haul: 3-115, 7-56 against New Zealand in Christchurch. Reaches quarter-final for Pakistan in the World Cup in India and Pakistan.

1996   Tours England, achieving 5-57 at Lord's and 6-78 at the Oval. Obtains his best ODI figures (5-36) against India in the Sahara Cup, Toronto. Then undergoes knee surgery, which keeps him out of the reckoning for Pakistan.

1996/97   Takes his 100th Test wicket (Bryan Young) against New Zealand in Rawalpindi.

1997   Named Wisden Cricketer of the Year in England.

1997/98   Takes his 150th Test wicket (Gary Kirsten) against South Africa in Durban.

1998/99   After a series of inconsistent performances, a persistent neck injury keeps him out of the Pakistan team. He leaves Somerset and returns to Pakistan.

1999/2000   Tours West Indies and Sri Lanka.

2000/01   Plays in ODI series against England in Pakistan. Tours New Zealand and England, but having been dropped from the Pakistan squad spends time playing for Northop Hall in Staffordshire, England.

2001/02   Captains National Bank to the Patron's Trophy in Pakistan.

2002   Plays for Little Stoke, an English League team. Then picks up a few matches with Surrey in the County Championship. Offered a contract with Sussex for 2003.

2003   Becomes the first bowler in five years to take over 100 wickets (103) in an English season. Sussex win the County Championship. Selected to play in Test series against South Africa in Pakistan.

2004   Leading wicket-taker in England with 84 wickets.

2005/06   Selected for Pakistan squad, but does not take the field against England in Pakistan.

2006   Takes 102 wickets in the County Championship as Sussex win the title again. In the crucial final game, against Notts, Mushtaq takes 13 wickets in the match, including career-best figures of nine for 48 in the second innings.

1

Twenty20

'If you want to be a good player you have to deliver on the cricket ground, not in the dressing-room'

22 June 2005. Five wickets for 11 runs from 3.3 overs.

As I ran down the changing room steps and on to the outfield at Hove, my mind was clear. I rejoiced that I had another opportunity to play the game I love and I was determined, as always, to do my best. The Sussex captain, Chris Adams, and coach, Peter Moores, had led the pre-match discussions and the bowlers were relaxed. In Twenty20 matches they always tell us the pressure is off the bowlers. We know we will get hit for lots of runs, especially us spinners, but we are prepared for that. Twenty20 is like the end of a longer version of cricket when a team has ten wickets in hand. Batsmen will not hesitate to go for their shots from the first ball, especially with the fielding restrictions that keep men in the ring for the first four overs.

It is far from easy to bowl slow balls with the shiny new ball as it can slip in the hand or roll off the fingers to give wides, short balls or full tosses. So Sussex always choose to open with James Kirtley and one of the overseas fast bowlers, such as Johan van der Wath or Rana Naved. We were told that Kirtley and van der Wath would bowl their first two overs, then Mark Davis and I would take over.

The team makes plans in the dressing-room before each innings. We will have already discussed the strengths of each opponent, but of course plans can soon change if the first over goes for 20 runs or wickets start to fall. Our coaches tell us that no matter what happens we must stay true to our own feelings and bowl in the way that feels comfortable for us on the day. Peter Moores encourages us to go into the nets before a game and bowl whatever we feel like bowling – changing the pace and length – just to get a rhythm and feel comfortable. Then, he says, stick with the type of balls that are working for you today.

I have my own plan for a Twenty20 match and it starts with the view that I am going to be hit and that I have to enjoy my bowling even when sixes and fours are flying around. What I will not do is allow myself to be hit around the ground without answering back. So if someone is playing a slog-sweep to the midwicket area I will bowl middle-and-leg and bowl straight, making sure that I do not stray outside the off stump, which would let the batsman free his arms. If the batsman tries to play me on the off side, say with a reverse sweep, I will try to bowl a little fuller or bowl more wrong 'uns (googlies). During the very first delivery you can see what the striker is looking to do and you have to read his body language. In Twenty20, decision-making by bowlers has to be very quick. Batsmen will try to fool you by looking to midwicket, but they actually want to reverse sweep you through third man for four; you have to adjust to that in a split second when you see the change in body position. When I come in to bowl I know that the batsmen are looking for my leg break, my flipper or the wrong 'un, but in Twenty20 I tend to stick with one ball, and it's the straight ball, or flipper. I do not try to spin the ball; I just keep it on middle-and-leg to stop them hitting freely. If someone is trying to use their feet to make space then I will put in a little leg break to let him know that the ball is spinning. But mostly I bowl straight and do not spin the ball. By the time the batsman has figured this out, I will have bowled three overs and only one remains! The batsmen will be frustrated because they will want to hit sixes, but will only be able to get singles. In Twenty20, to go for 30 runs off four overs is pretty good, but I might only have gone for 13 or 14 off the first three overs; if I can do this I'm delighted, because the batsmen do not fear getting out as they do in the longer game and I know that I am winning the mental battle against them.

Some people thought that Twenty20 cricket would destroy the longer version of the game, but I think it is brilliant. We know that the crowds are flocking to matches, and that has to be a good thing, but it also helps players with the longer one-day and three- and four-day games. Perhaps it does not help batsmen technically because in Twenty20 they have to chase the ball, but professional players have to be clever and adapt to situations quicker than ordinary players so this type of game has an important role to play in developing decision-making skills. Underachievers often fail to make the grade because they do not adapt to changing conditions quickly enough; they practise the same thing over and over and seem to be quite good, but when conditions change in a match they cannot adapt. Twenty20 is so fast and things change so quickly that players have to use their brains. If they learn to use their brains quickly in Twenty20, it will help them to become cleverer all-round cricketers.

The Twenty20 game has brought a lot of technology into cricket, but nothing can replace the human brain. I have watched many great cricketers throughout my career and tried to learn from them. In the case of the greatest, such as Imran Khan and Ian Botham, the hours in the nets have provided the technique but the factor that makes them special is their decision-making and clever use of their brains. Although I've said that batsmen do not fear getting out in Twenty20, I believe that any batsman who gets 40 or more runs should go on to make a big innings, just as they should in the longer game. I've often seen batsmen get aggressive and start hitting boundaries, but they do not realise that they will be out if they try to play every shot like that. They should understand that the fielding team is happy for them to get singles, so after a couple of boundaries they should go for a few singles and preserve their wicket. Once they are out, the new batsman has to face a few balls before he will score runs. So, if you hit a six and then try for another and get out, the over may end up as 6 for one. But if you hit a six then content yourself with singles and twos, the over may produce 10 or 11 and you will have kept your wickets in hand.

Some bowlers think very negatively. If the wicket is good and the batsman is playing well, you must stay disciplined, stick to your own game and try to out-think him. Maybe you bowl him a couple of balls so he can get some runs and feel more comfortable about you.

If you let him have 8 runs or so he will relax and think that he does not have to play defensively, then – BANG! Put in a variety ball. I love it when a batsman starts to get confident and plays me like a seamer because I know that I can put in a leg break or a wrong 'un and he'll be off his guard. If I get hit for six, I just think about how I am going to get him out next ball. If I started to worry about going for another six, my body language would show him that he is winning and give him confidence. I will not allow that to happen.

Negative thinking can even include worrying about the weather. Sky Sports were covering a day/nighter and the interviewer said, 'It's very cold today and I don't think this weather suits your fingers.' He did have a point, as it's true that spinners struggle when the weather is cold as it is harder to grip the ball, but I said to him, 'If I start thinking about the weather and the fact that it isn't good for me and my kind of deliveries, I will find that I cannot perform in the match. I cannot think that the weather is bad. I have to think that I will prove once more that I can bowl and the weather is OK.' You can tell when the captain is about to throw the ball to you, so I prepare for my spell by talking to myself in the field. I tell myself that my fingers are warm and I am going to turn the ball and play a major role in the game.

Essex had elected to bat and Kirtley and van der Wath had bowled two overs each when I was brought in to the attack. I knew that the wicket would spin and was determined to change the pace of each ball. Variation is very important in Twenty20 cricket. You must keep the batsman guessing – if one ball is 50mph and the next 70mph and you keep changing the pace, it will take away his timing and unsettle him throughout his innings.

Andy Flower had been run out, but his brother Grant was at the crease. I bowled a couple of straight balls to him, then Grant came down the wicket and tried to hit me over the top. This one was a leg break; he missed it and was stumped by Tim Ambrose.

Ryan ten Doeschate was caught and bowled. In any kind of cricket you can hit or pull a short ball, but he was looking to sweep so I took the pace off the ball. He started to go for a sweep, but when he saw that the ball was shorter he tried to flick it through midwicket. He did not spot that the ball was slower so he was through with his shot too quickly and he edged it straight back to me.

As usual I had set my own field, with five men on the leg side and four men on the off. When Foster came in, the first ball he faced was a wrong 'un. He could clearly see how the field looked and decided to try to play a reverse sweep to the next ball. I spotted this and knew why – he felt that if he could beat the one slip he could get a boundary. So I bowled him a straight fuller ball. If it had just been on a good length he would have been able to see it early, free his arms and take a swing at it. A thick top edge would carry over the slip. With the fuller ball, his timing would have to be perfect. He could have taken a single to the leg side, but he was looking for more runs and I was looking for an lbw. On this occasion it was my day: the second time I bowled the same ball, he missed it and the umpire gave him leg before.

My first couple of balls to Andre Adams were slow leg breaks. Although he could have come forward and played them off the front foot, he went back and played me into the covers for no runs. This told me how he was thinking, so I bowled a quicker ball. He went back again, but missed it and was given out leg before.

Danish Kaneria played three balls of my last over. He blocked the first, a leg break. The second one was a wrong 'un and he blocked it again. He was bringing his front foot very far forward so I thought, 'Why not bowl a little shorter, but a little quicker?' I bowled a quick straight ball, which he missed and was clean bowled. I had my five wickets.

I was amazed to have done so well, especially as Essex had been going so well at the start of the innings. They were looking good to get 140 or 150 runs. The crowd and my team-mates were delighted. Someone commented that this was the first Twenty20 'five-for' in the club. Then I was told that five for 11 was a national record. Everyone was predicting that this record was going to stay forever, but I said, 'No, the record is always there to be broken. If God can give me five for 11, he can do the same for someone else.' To be honest, I was not reckoning on anyone getting more wickets to set a new record, but rather that five for 9 or 10 would be possible with the new ball.

The next day I heard that Tim Murtagh had taken six for 24 and thought, well, there you go, the record has gone; but I was still satisfied that I had been first to 'five' and that I had gone for fewer runs.

Sussex played Surrey in the following match and I found Tim in the dining room. I went up to him and said, 'Look, I'm not happy with you.' He said, 'Why?' and I told him, 'You broke my record and an old fellow like me should have a least one record at the end of his career.' He said, 'Mushy, someone else will do it to me!' and he was right. I congratulated him and we both enjoyed the moment. Enjoying the moment is not something that has always come easily in my career, and I am glad that now I face success and disappointment with equal contentment.

I hope that the story of my journey to this point and the help that I have received in finding the right direction will inspire you as much as it has inspired me. I have been a first-class cricketer for almost twenty years and my world has changed from very humble beginnings through a worldwide adventure that has brought me back to my family and my faith.

2

Early Days

'I was brought up to believe that you should live for the day because you never know what may happen tomorrow.'

Mushtaq Ahmed. Born: June 28 1970, Sahiwal, Pakistan.

My parents had ten children, five boys and five girls, but I lost a brother and a sister during childhood. So I grew up in a family with four sisters and three brothers. My father, Shamsudin, had to work all the hours under the sun to support us. He would often start at five o'clock in the morning and not return before midnight, as he was labouring at a cotton factory but was also responsible for getting the other labourers that the factory needed – for this he earned £1 a day. When he died in 2003, some people from the factory came to his funeral and they said to me, 'Do you know why you have been successful, Mushtaq?' I said, 'No'. They said, 'Twenty-five years your father worked with us and we never had a problem with a single penny. He was a very honest man.' It was then I realised that God will look after you sooner or later. If you stay honest, it may be that you will not get everything you need, but God will take care of your children or your family. My father did not see that life, but his family has felt the blessings of Allah. All now run their own lives and have jobs and businesses, but this is all because of the example set by my father. I cannot express the depth of my feelings towards him. He was a brave man and the perfect role model of a father. He gave me pride and the mental attitude I needed to be successful in sport. Everything he did was for his family and I miss him every day. Since I lost him I appreciate him more and more and pray to Allah to give my father everything he needs in heaven.

We lived in a district called Sahiwal, which is about two and a half hours' drive from Lahore. Although the population of the district numbers over 200,000 there was no major industrial or commercial centre. In terms of technology and facilities it was almost a village. The main products were cows, buffalo and cotton. Most of the population lived rural lives and we kept three buffaloes in our yard. We had to feed them with hay and straw and they supplied us with milk each day. Our house only had three rooms and all the children would sleep in one of them. We relied entirely on my father's work at the cotton mill for money. He would always spend his wages the same day he got them on food and clothing. My parents made sure we ate properly every day. This is an important part of our Muslim faith. We are taught not to worry about tomorrow. We take care of our needs today and trust that God will provide for the next day. My father would read the Qur'an every day and tell us always to follow the right direction by following God's orders and by using the Prophet's life as an example.

My mother stayed at home and took care of the family. We were part of a wider family, with uncles and cousins in the same area. The culture of families in Pakistan is very close; we share our sadness and happiness and provide for each other whenever we can. We are lucky to have such a tradition where there is a lot of support. People would not have a bank account or keep money for themselves; they share it with their family. When I first earned money I would give it straight to my father, who would distribute it to other members of the family.

My father had not really had much of an education and he was determined that his children should not go down the same path. He thought we should study hard at school and he was extremely annoyed when my cricket constantly got in the way of my school work.. The problem I faced was that we did not know anyone who was involved in cricket so my father thought there was no future in sport. He was a good role model and a hard-working man and I feel very lucky to have had him as a father; however, he deeply disapproved of me playing cricket as a youngster and would often beat me if he found I was falling behind or missing my studies because of my love of cricket. He would tell me that if I did not get an education I would end up as a labourer like him and he was frightened that I might lose the opportunity to go on to better things. One day, one of my father's cousins said to him, 'You are destroying your son. Do not let him waste his time playing cricket. He should get an education or do some technical work.' He felt so strongly that I should get an education, but no matter how much my father shouted at or beat me, I had a passion for cricket and would not stop playing. People talk about being focused for twenty-four hours a day and it is often an exaggeration, but for me it was true. Sometimes I would practise through the night!

As a youngster, I played cricket in the streets for hours on end. At the time Pakistan had a great hockey team and Abdul Qadir was our cricketing hero. Boys only knew about those two sports so I learned to play hockey and wanted to be a hockey star. Then Imran became captain of the Pakistan cricket team and I, along with many other boys, practised being a cricketer whilst dreaming of becoming a famous sportsman. Gradually cricket became my passion. Although we did not own a TV I would watch cricket whenever I could and was quick to imitate the players I admired. I would never be without a cricket ball in my hand and would happily bowl a ball at a poplar tree for hours on end. I imagined I was Imran Khan bowling medium-pace or Abdul Qadir bowling his leg-spin. For me the tree was the stumps and I was in a Test match. If I missed the tree I had to run after the ball before going through the motions again – so it taught me to be accurate! All I wanted to do was play cricket. I would be late for meals and as soon as I finished school I would throw my books in the house to go out and play. I even used to sleep with a cricket ball. My mum could not understand it and some people said I was unstable. I should tell you that the 'cricket' balls we used at this time were not the kind of ball I am used to using now. If we managed to get hold of a tennis ball we would use that, but they were very expensive. Sometimes we would put a cheap plastic football into very hot water until it melted and shrank to the size of a cricket ball. These balls had a lot of bounce and could be bowled with some pace. That was the kind of ball I bowled at the tree.

Some days I skipped school altogether. I would find where people were playing cricket and go and join in. They never let me bowl or bat so I just fielded for them. I missed a lot of schooling; at one stage, I must have missed 20 days of school and the teacher eventually called my father to ask where I had been. It must have been very embarrassing for him because he believed I had been attending classes and was shocked to find out I had not been there for such a long time. My father took me aside and asked me, 'How is your education going?' I said, 'Fine, absolutely brilliant. I'm doing a great job at school.' So he said, 'Well, as you're doing such a good job, why not have extra tuition after school so you can really succeed?' I said, 'No, I really don't need it.' I was feeling really guilty and I knew I was in big trouble when he took me on his bike to see the teacher. They both beat me until one of the sticks actually broke on me.

My determination to play cricket caused arguments between my parents. My father blamed my mother for giving me too much freedom, while for her part she asked how she could be expected to discipline me when I didn't even listen to my father. It was a tough upbringing in many ways, but it has made me and my elder brother and sisters tough and helps us cope with difficult situations today; we have gained very strong minds from our father.

Although my father did not support my cricketing activity as a youngster, I think my enthusiasm for sport came through him because he played a lot of Kabaddi in local competitions. For our holidays we used to travel to a very primitive village near Sialkot on the border with India (where lots of cricket equipment and footballs are made). This village played host to a Kabaddi tournament, and my father would play there with my uncles. As children we watched them and my uncles would say, 'This is a proper game. You should play this. This is a man's game.' They really did not have a clue about cricket. When I did start to play cricket seriously, my father would feed me like a Kabaddi player because he thought I would need the same bulk and body strength. We had buffaloes at home and my father would give me milk every night and morning and put eggs into the milk to make me strong. He would say, 'If you have strength you will be able to play good cricket.' But I had to tell him, 'You don't need this kind of strength to play cricket. You need to have mental strength and to be clever. If you are light you can move quickly in the field and this makes you a better cricketer.' My father used to say, 'No, I don't believe that. Strength is everything.'

My father and my uncles were always strong. I never saw them panic or worry about events around them. It may be because of the security they created that I was able to deal with situations that would have terrified other people – and would terrify me now! When I was about sixteen there was a terrible storm one night. We had electricity, but there was a power cut (as there often was) so my sister came into the bedroom, where the other children were sleeping, with a candle. When she looked up she saw the ceiling was cracking and giving way. She called to us and we all rushed out of the room. Shortly after, the whole room collapsed.

It was a very lucky escape. If she had not come in with the candle, we would have been killed. I can still remember my mum crying with shock and relief. I was just excited and could not wait to tell everyone at school the next day about our lucky escape. I repeated the story many times, with more passion each time.

I was not a reckless boy, but I did take risks, simply because I had such enthusiasm for life and for cricket. One moment as a youngster I will never forget was when the West Indies toured Pakistan and played against the Rest of Punjab at Sahiwal. I saw it as my only chance to see some of my heroes in action, and nothing was going to stop me watching the likes of Viv Richards, Gordon Greenidge and Malcolm Marshall. My cousin and I told our parents we were going to school and then shot off to the match, although we did not have any money for a ticket. It would have been a very long walk to the match if we followed the road and crossed the railway bridge, so we took a shortcut across the railway track to save time. The trains were in the station and we ran underneath a train in the process of pulling out of the station. Looking back, it was so dangerous; if one of us had slipped we could easily have been killed. I just did not think about it at the time; that was my passion for the game.

When we came to the ground there were massive queues and we had no money for a ticket. There were lots of police around, but I knew something would happen and we would get into the ground one way or another. We hung around outside and ran backwards and forwards trying to get a glimpse whilst looking for a way in. Fortunately, one of the policemen saw us running around the ground and he helped get us in some time after the match had started. I was not disappointed. I can remember Sylvester Clarke storming in and bowling bouncers. It really made me want to play in such a game one day. It was a fabulous experience, even for such a short time, and we stayed behind afterwards to catch any glimpse of any of the West Indians we could. For me it was like being at the World Cup final; it was an amazing feeling.

As a young teenager I was a good fielder and could run quickly between the wickets, but I was not a great batsman or bowler. Once I began to perform well, scoring lots of runs and taking wickets, the teachers would sometimes let me out of lessons to practise for half an hour, although I usually went missing for a couple of hours. We did not have a television at home, but fortunately one of our neighbours owned a set and I would go to his house to watch cricket whenever I could. They were quite happy with the arrangement because they would send me on errands, going to the cleaners or collecting the milk, and I would run as fast as I could to finish the job and get back to watch the game. I spent hours in front of that TV watching Imran Khan. I could imitate Imran Khan's run up, to all my friends' delight, and was the only boy in the neighbourhood – and later the cricket club – who could reproduce Abdul Qadir's run up and technique. Abdul Qadir was my bowling hero. I just loved seeing him bowl and marvelled at the way he would mesmerise batsmen. At that age I was already observing cricketers very closely and analysing their move-ments. I would watch him produce his variations and then go out and try them for myself. By copying what I saw and practising for hours I found that the other boys in the street could not play me and I was getting them out. It was not long before they were telling me to stop bowling like that and just bowl with pace instead. This told me that I must be doing something right, so I persevered with leg-spin. I was always asking questions and this was an important time in my cricketing career when I progressed very quickly.

The primary school I went to was very poor and we could not always sit in a classroom. We were sometimes taught underneath trees and things did not get much better when I went to the local Mahmuddiah High School at the age of eleven. There was virtually no sports equipment and little chance of progressing further. I was quite a good hockey player at school and played at centre-forward. My brother Ishfaq was vice-captain and put me in the team when they were short one day. I was little, quick and good at dribbling. After watching me play hockey one of my sports teachers thought I could help the cricket team when they were a player short for an upcoming match. He asked me if I would be twelfth man and I agreed very happily. At the nets before the match they asked me to bowl at the batsmen and I bowled leg breaks. I was spinning the ball big time and getting wickets. So the teachers picked me to play and I used to pick up three or four wickets every game.

School cricket was very important even for our poor school. The headmaster would declare the school closed for the match and every student had to go to the ground to watch. The players felt like heroes at the age of thirteen as there was always a big crowd. Some parents would give us money as we left the pitch and we might get 300 or 400 rupees each when we divided it up at the dinner after the match. It might not seem very much, but getting 30 rupees or more, which was only about 30 pence, made a big difference to us. In school the next day the students and the teachers would talk about the match and show us great respect if we had done well.

My father eventually relented after I had been playing for a couple of years and he offered me his unconditional support. It was a wonderful moment for me when he took me on his bicycle to the nearest shop selling cricket gear. I was about thirteen years old and he bought me a cricket bat for 300 rupees, which was about £3 at the time. This was a lot of money for him and it meant everything to me. I showed it to everyone for days and went on to use the bat for the next couple of years. My father then started to watch me play and enjoyed the games, but I felt immense pressure when he was there and I struggled to get the same satisfaction as before. I would be very scared and it affected me so much that I asked him to stop coming to watch me. I felt that if I failed I was letting him down and would be a disappointment to him. He agreed to stop watching me but, little did I know, he was actually turning up and viewing games from a distance or even from behind a tree.

My big break came when we played against our local rivals, the Comprehensive High School, in the district final. This was a two-day match against a much better-equipped and richer school. We were never expected to win and we did lose the match, but I managed to take four for 80 off my 25 overs. Our fielding was not very good and a lot of the decisions did not go our way as we were the little school, but I did enough for the opposition to approach me with an offer to go and play for them. I did not know what to do but my teacher, Master Shafriq, advised that if I wanted to progress then I needed access to good facilities and to play at as high a level as possible. The Comprehensive School offered to buy me a bicycle because they were situated nearly four miles away, and I decided to make the move.

Another important thing happened to me during that game. The opposition had a really quick left-arm bowler and we had no helmets. I have to admit I was really scared, and he got me out for a duck. After the game I was told that there was no point playing cricket if you were scared. I learned to toughen myself up and I remain a firm believer in facing up to reality. My coach, and later on my father, would tell me if I was bowling badly and I would be a harsh critic of myself. They told me that if I was honest with myself then I could be honest with everyone, so I was very self-critical, but I also learned that there is no point in worrying about failure or the opposition.

I had to wear a clean uniform and polished shoes for my new school. The building was like a palace compared to the school I had attended, but I suffered a terrible start as I was like a fish out of water. On the first day I heard two boys talking and I thought, 'Hang on, what language are they speaking?' They spoke in an educated way and they used some English, too. In my district doctors and lawyers are very important and we could never imagine having such a career, but these boys were discussing their ambition to be doctors as if it were the most natural thing in the world. There was no freedom at all and I was not used to such discipline. We had to park our bicycles in a special place and our shoes were checked in assembly each morning. For three or four days the boys treated me as if I was not a nice person, because it was clear that I was uneducated. We spoke Punjabi at home, which is a strong dialect that is not spoken or taught in school and I was not allowed to read or write in it. The official language of the school and country was Urdu. This is a more 'refined' language and my accent set me apart. For a while I did not fit in at school and my old friends resented the fact that I had left them. When I saw them they would say, 'Mushy is easy to buy,' because I had moved. In some ways I regretted moving away from my loving school and friends – we had nothing, but really looked after each other.

Once cricket practice began, I was able to show that I had talent and the boys began to accept me. The teacher who took me there, Attar Rahman, always showed his belief in me and he advised me to do some reading too, as education would help my cricket. I was very nervous when I first went there, but I started to turn in some good performances with bat and ball. I began to relax; gradually everyone became friendly and the teachers gave me respect because of my cricketing ability. I had made the decision to join the school for my own future, and eventually everyone agreed that I had made the right decision.

I became popular at school when I was about fourteen. The Comprehensive High School made me their captain and, all of a sudden, the boys from rich families started to show me respect. It was then that I was invited to play for Montgomery Cricket Club. This was a big club in Pakistan with excellent facilities. The club was owned by Bisharat Shafi, who ran a biscuit and sweet factory. He was a powerful man and also the president of the Multan Cricket Division, and he said that if I played well for his club then I would get my chance with Multan. We had been doing well at school level, and I was also playing on Fridays for Montgomery. Some days the temperature reached 40–45°C, but I continued to train and practise hard. The effort paid off when I was selected to play for the first XI with players like Manzoor Elahi, who later played in a memorable match against an England touring side.

I was only fifteen when I was first selected for Multan Under-19s. We played against the big cities like Lahore and Karachi, so it was a real step up in class and it took me away from Sahiwal. In my first season I was more of a batsman than a bowler and I did very well. At that time, I had no idea how to bowl a wrong 'un or the flipper properly and I think people saw my talent as lying more in my batting. The management at Multan backed me all the way through this period, and by the time I was sixteen I had been selected for my first-class debut against Hyderabad. My selection did not go down too well with a lot of the established members of the side, who felt I was getting preferential treatment. To be honest, I was not good enough for first-class cricket at the time. There were many other players who were better-equipped and I could understand why a lot of them were unhappy with me. Although I did not deserve to play on my ability, the coach and management liked me because I was a really hard worker. I would happily spend all day at the cricket ground. I usually turned up at two o'clock – two hours before the official start time – to practise before each game; the other players would not arrive until the temperature had begun to drop.

When my coach was not around, the senior players would give me a hard time. They would make me fetch water for them and ask me why I was playing, but it did not worry me – I saw it as part of the learning process. Although I understood why my team-mates were angry, I thought they were wrong to take it out on me personally. However, I was very shy and still respected my elders, even if I did not agree with their way of thinking. The whole experience made me tougher and I learnt patience. I continued to respect the older players even though they treated me badly because I felt, as they had played a lot of first-class cricket, they had earned respect from youngsters.

I scored 75 on my debut for Multan, while another youngster named Inzamam-ul-Haq scored a 100 on the same day. I could see by their body language that some of the players were not at all happy and they were worried I was going to take their place, but other people within the club made me feel welcome.

I continued to play at under-19s level and it was here that I really learned to become the bowler I am today. I used to get hammered a lot when I was young, but the coach would frequently get me to come back and bowl at the tail-enders to help build my confidence. I would quite often have figures of none for 100, but end up with three or four wickets for 120. This tactic helped me a lot at that stage in my career and it was nice to get a few wickets in my pocket.

I was made captain of Multan under-19s when I was sixteen and had a couple of useful players under my command: Inzi and a young up-and-coming quick bowler named Waqar Younis. I actually got into quite a bit of trouble with the club management over a decision I made with Inzi during one match – I felt a little bit guilty about the good treatment I was receiving, so I let Inzi have my batting place at number 4 instead of 5. When the coach found out, he went absolutely crazy and asked me why I gave someone else my place in the batting order. He slapped me about for disobeying his instructions; while no coach should ever do that, I accepted it because I knew he had my interests at heart.

At this time, my career was really on a roll. I was captain of the under-19s and playing first-class cricket. My name was recognised by other teams and I was living a dream come true, but I would never have believed what was around the corner.

I did not expect to represent Pakistan at the age of seventeen. In fact nothing was further from my mind when, after the 1987 World Cup, England came to Sahiwal in December to play against a Punjab Chief Minister's XI made up of youngsters or out-of-form first-class players. As I was a local lad, Basharat Shafi asked me to be the water-boy for the Punjab side. My duties basically were to look after the side and carry the kit for them. I was named as the 14th member of the side, but I was not really part of the squad; I was just there to help out and for the experience of the dressing-room on a big-match occasion. Salim Malik was the captain, as he was looking for some practice before the forthcoming Test matches. I was sitting on the ground watching the England players with all their smart equipment, spikes and sunglasses. On the other side of the ground were the players I was looking after, some of whom would go on to play

for Pakistan. Then I noticed Salim Malik, a superstar, in nego-
tiations with the management; he came over to me and said,
'Mushtaq, young fellow, you are playing today.' I was speechless. I
was truly amazed. I marvelled that I was going to be playing against
John Emburey, Derek Randall and David Capel. I kept telling
myself I was going to play in a match with Tim Robinson! I was not
nervous – I was flying. I did not even have my kit with me and I had
not brought any spikes.

It was only my second or third first-class match and I never found
out why I was picked. I know it is the usual policy to choose a couple
of the local youngsters but we had a very good left-arm spinner called
Bilal Rana at the time. He is one of the best all-rounders I have come
across in Pakistan and he only missed out on international recognition because he had a bad accident during his career. He really
deserved to play in this match. He was full of confidence and loved
to bowl when things were tough. I was always very impressed with
him. However, for some reason I got the nod, along with Manzoor
Elahi who went on to play two Tests for Pakistan. I was absolutely
thrilled and it never entered my head that I was taking someone
else's place.

It was an incredible game. I bowled 36 overs and took six for 85
in the first innings, and I remember dismissing Tim Robinson, Bill
Athey, Dave Capel and Phil DeFreitas. When I came off the pitch,
there were cameras flashing everywhere and the English media were
asking me to stand to one side and have my photo taken. I was
overwhelmed. It was an experience I will never forget, especially as I
had turned up really only to hold the drinks.

Within days, the fairytale continued. Abdul Qadir had fallen out
with the Pakistan Cricket Board and it was in the news that I had
been called up for the Third Test against England in Karachi. I
cannot even begin to express my feelings. I had dreamt about this
moment all my life and it was really happening – and so quickly. The
icing on the cake came when the manager of United Bank called to
offer me a first-class full-time contract with his side. United Bank
had a reputation for developing good young players and they had
many big names in their team. The manager offered me a job as a

Field Officer, which meant that all I had to do was play cricket and I would be paid 2,500 rupees a month. This was a huge amount of money for me at the time and, needless to say, I jumped at the chance. I called my parents and said, 'I've got a bank job. I can bring money home and support the family.' I was used to taking all the cheques and prize money from cricket to my father. I used to eat only what I needed and save the daily food allowance I received to take home to my brother. This was a huge achievement for our family and I was thrilled that I would be able to repay my father's love in this way.

Javed Miandad and Mudassar Nazar were the captain and vice-captain of Pakistan and they were a great help during the net sessions, but I felt like I was in a jungle. I was standing next to my heroes in the nets or sitting next to them in the dressing-room. I was fighting for my place against the likes of Iqbal Qasim and Tauseef Ahmed. Javed seemed very keen to put me into the side for the match, but I then heard that Abdul Qadir had resolved his differences with the management and had caught a late night flight to join up with the squad and take his place in the team. Was I disappointed? Not really. I was not even sure where I was for the first few days. I was happy enough just spending time with these players and had not even started to think about actually playing in the match.

I signed the contract with United Bank and was released from the Pakistan team to make my debut with my new team-mates. I think we played against Agricultural Bank and I remember taking four wickets and scoring 40-odd runs in the first innings. They were very happy with me and every day seemed to be better than the one before, particularly as I was earning professional money. As I mixed with the great players, I also began to learn what freedom was all about. For the five or six years that I had been learning the game in Sahiwal I had devoted myself to my coach. I had often visited his house after school and I did jobs for him just to try to learn from him, but he was very strict and would often beat me. I did not know any better and it did not seem to be too bad for me, but he was oppressive, he did not allow me to express myself, and as a result I had no confidence. I was frightened to make mistakes because I thought that my coach would be angry with me. In our culture we believe that older people should always be respected, so I would just listen and never question my coach. One of the United Bank players who came from Sahiwal taught me that it was right to respect your coach, but you did not have to accept everything he does or says. The top players helped me find a way to talk with coaches and to ask questions, whilst at the same time maintaining your respect for them.

The events of 1987 took me into a new world. My horizons expanded beyond anything I had previously experienced and I have fond memories of everyone who supported me as I made the transition from a naïve young schoolboy to a professional cricketer.

3

The Pakistan Cricket Scene

'The biggest problem Pakistan has is the lack of facilities. Some
first-class grounds do not even have toilets. It is astonishing that
you can play a first-class game, preparing to play for your country,
in these circumstances . . .'

Few people seem to know much about cricket in Pakistan, so I
thought I would spend a few moments explaining the scene so you
can understand a little more about the environment from which so
many great cricketers have emerged.

There are fourteen associations who play in the Quaid-e-Azam
trophy between October and November each year, divided into two
divisions. In the Gold Division 2005/06 are: Faisalabad, Sialkot,
Rawalpindi, Lahore Shalimar, Peshawar, Karachi Urban, and
Multan (my first team). The Silver Division features: Karachi
Harbour, Hyderabad, Lahore Ravi, Quetta, Islamabad, Abbottabad.
The Pakistan Cricket Board supports the associations and the teams
select their players from the club sides. It is an honour to be selected
and it also pays quite well. At the moment players can earn 10,000
rupees per match.

Once a player has represented his association, his next ambition is
to play for one of the department teams in the Patron's Trophy
which takes place between December and March. There are two
divisions in the Patron's Trophy and in 2005/06 the teams are:
Division A: Pakistan International Airlines, Habib Bank, Khan
Research Laboratories, Sui Northern Gas Pipelines and Pakistan
Customs. Division B: Pakistan Telecommunication Company,
National Bank of Pakistan, Water and Power Development
Authority, Zarai Taraqiati Bank and Service Industries. As you can

see, big companies own all the teams. This brings money into the game, but when businesses decide to pull out the teams disappear.

Both trophy competitions consist of a series of matches with the top two in each division playing in the semi-finals. There is also a one-day series that follows the same pattern. Only the semi-finals and final games at Lahore and Karachi draw a big crowd. Other matches are played in front of few spectators, unless the international players are available. The fact is, the economy is such that most potential spectators are trying to earn a living and cannot afford to go to many matches. However, Twenty20 cricket is now a feature of the season from January to March and 35,000 watched the 2006 final between Faisalabad Wolves and Sialkot Stallions. The crowd enjoyed free entry which is a great help in making the game more popular, but many genuine cricket fans did not get into the game and a number of younger 'fans' behaved badly, throwing bottles and stones at players and ripping out seating. Sialkot eventually won, but the game was interrupted for a long time and did not finish until 2.35 a.m.!

Sometimes department sides play three-day matches against association teams; it is in these matches that good players are able to make a name for themselves and hope to be offered a trial with one of the senior teams. The trials can last for a month or so before a decision is made.

All I ever wanted to do was play first-class cricket so I could get a job in a bank. The companies would give you a permanent job if you were a good enough cricketer, rather than a short-term contract. So, for someone like me with no real education, first-class cricket was a way to guarantee a future. My brothers and sisters worked hard at school, but it became clear to my father that he would have to support my cricket, as this would be the only way I could do something with my life. Thankfully, I was signed by United Bank. I would have struggled to find a job in a bank, as there are plenty of men and women graduates applying for every job. Once I had a contract with United Bank, I believed that they would look after me for life. Other cricketers who could barely read, write or do mathematics had jobs for life with the bank, as they would be kept on as players and coaches for the bank teams in the local leagues.

School cricket in Pakistan was very tough and very competitive. When the school team played, all the students were expected to go to the match. The pressure was intense. The pressure continued as I rose through club cricket and first-class cricket – domestic cricket in Pakistan is the toughest cricket I've ever played. Spinners have a really hard time because so many batsmen in Pakistan can take you apart quite easily.

When I first played club cricket for Montgomery I looked on those men who played for Multan as heroes. The few who were then selected by the banks were absolute stars. We would watch them in the nets wearing their 'Habib Bank' or 'United Bank' tracksuits and caps. They walked around as if they were stars and we all wanted to emulate them. It was from watching them that I took the attitude that I had to 'sell' myself to the big teams. I had to show them that I would be the diamond in their side!

The 1980s was a time of massive passion and enthusiasm for cricket among the poorer people of Pakistan. Ninety per cent of first-class cricketers in Pakistan could not afford a bag or whites, so they relied on the patronage of their clubs; if not, they had to borrow clothing and equipment. I know that Inzamam, Waqar, Saeed Anwar and myself owe our enduring success with Pakistan to our upbringing. We were not playing at being cricketers like some of the rich people who managed a couple of seasons in the first-class game before going back into business. We were fighting for survival and developed the strong characters and resolve needed to stay at the top once we managed to get there.

When I began at Montgomery Biscuit Factory they would give me 500 rupees a month, which I was able to spend on cricket gear. The rich people at the club, some of whom knew nothing about cricket really, were keen to see young people playing, especially if they thought that we were good enough to ensure victory for their club. I am very grateful for the help they gave me. I could not afford to pay the 50 rupees needed to use the nets, for example, but the club patrons would help me out and it was their help that enabled me to go on to represent my country.

Despite the fact that many grounds were in poor shape, the wickets were usually quite good. Now, as the game becomes more professional, facilities are improving, but I can also see that much of the passion that came from our impoverished upbringing is being lost. It is important that sportspeople are well-rewarded, but I am not happy to see so many young fellows in many sports getting paid huge amounts of money as soon as they achieve some success; I think this makes them too comfortable and too selfish. Their passion can drain away and they can lose a proper perspective on life. People who get too much too early lose sight of their real goals. In Pakistan there are many academies now, and funding for sports development is readily available, but I am not sure that making life easy for youngsters is the answer to everything. In my view, you have to fall over at least five or six times before you can learn to run!

4

Culture Clashes

'If you want to learn something, you have to be patient. When the Somerset captain first spoke to me I used to pick up one word and then have to guess the rest. In this way I tried to grasp what he was on about. To be honest, I'm still doing it!'

Looking back, it must have been hilarious to watch this seventeen-year-old country boy make his way on to the national and international scene. I was completely overwhelmed by the situation and did not have a clue what was going on. The trip from Lahore to Karachi in preparation for the Third Test was my first time on an aeroplane. I found the whole episode very confusing and did not even know how to fasten my seatbelt. We are very casual about the safety announcements on aeroplanes nowadays, but I needed to be taught everything during that trip. Things went from bad to worse when I arrived at the top-class team hotel in Karachi. As the rest of the side went about their business, I waited in the lobby and was given the key to a second-floor room. I noticed that everyone was using the lift so I followed suit with my two bags, but when I got into the compartment I realised I did not know how to use it; I just kept going up and down and finding myself back on the ground floor. I could see that people were beginning to wonder why I was not going to my room. This happened a few times before Wasim Akram noticed I was having a few problems. He came over and introduced himself and congratulated me on my recent spell against England. Wasim looked at my key and showed me how to use the lift, which was a great relief at the time because it was a more nerve-wracking experience than bowling against England. For the young Mushy, this was my first taste of the big time and I was in a new and alien world.

My cricket career had begun to develop in 1987 and the New Year continued where the old one had left off as I was selected for the Under-19 World Cup in Adelaide. They picked another leg-spinner named Manzoor Ali from Karachi in the provisional 24-man squad. He was a big name because he had been playing professionally for two years, and I believed that the Under-19 selectors thought he was a better player than me. I could see it in their body language. However, my wicket-taking spell against England helped me a lot and I think that is what won them over, as Manzoor did not make the final squad. Winning the selectors over was a big boost for my confidence and my family were very happy that I had been selected to go on the tour. Inzamam and Waqar failed to make the provisional squad but Inzi hit three consecutive tons for Multan and received a late call-up. Although I was delighted with my selection and progress, this was a worrying time for me because I knew that I would be travelling abroad for the first time. Even worse, it was to an English-speaking country and I could not speak a word of the language. As the leaving date loomed I looked at my Pakistan blazer with the star and the moon badge and I could not stop smiling with pride. Unfortunately, the blazer was to receive some well-meaning but disasterous treatment at the hands of my younger sister, Zaneet, when I returned from the World Cup. She wanted to show her pride and love for me by washing the blazer ready for a photograph I was due to have with my club, Montgomery. We did not own any 'Western' clothes so she assumed that the blazer could be hand-washed, scrubbed and wrung out just as she laundered our simple cotton clothes. When she had finished the jacket had completely lost its shape and the buttons were no longer in a straight line. I took it to the dry cleaners and asked them to sort it out. They did their best, but could not get it back into perfect shape. I had no choice but to wear it for the photograph. Sadly, my appearance did not really match my achievements at that time.

The U-19 squad was split into groups of two players and each pair had to stay with an Australian family. I stayed in a small town named

Mildura, outside Adelaide, with Inzi, who was less confident in his English than I was, if that were possible. The house belonged to the Tipping family but, as you can imagine, communication was not great to start with. We managed to make ourselves understood with a lot of hand signals but the poor family must have wondered what they had let themselves in for. Naturally, they served us English-style food and gave us knives and forks. We were used to sitting on a mat and using our hands to eat. This is the most natural way to eat food and I did not even know how to hold a knife and fork. We tried to copy our adopted parents and they understood our problems and were very kind to us. Unfortunately, they did seem to give us small portions of food and we did not like to ask for any more. We just grabbed as much bread as we could off the table at each meal. After two nights, we were very hungry and went on a night raid to the fridge while they slept. We ate all the ice cream and fruit in the fridge! The next day, the Tippings went to Wasim Raja, our manager, and explained that we just needed to let them know if we wanted more food. Wasim said the family really cared about us and we should try and communicate as slowly as possible. It meant a lot to us that they were concerned for our wellbeing, and for the rest of our time with them they did everything they could to help us adjust to this different way of life. In fact, they were very good role models. They would take us swimming, to the river, beach or the shops and show us how to enjoy life. We treated them as parents and I remember offering to give Mr Tipping a foot and head massage, as that is what we would do with our parents back home. He was amazed when I told him this and joked that he would get on the next plane to Pakistan if he could expect this each day. We had barbecue parties and formed a very close bond with the family. I looked forward to going home to see my parents at the end of our stay, but I was very disappointed to leave the Tippings. I remember quite a few of the players crying when they had to leave their new families.

From Mildura we went to Adelaide to play the semi-final and the Australian Cricket Board arranged new hosts for us. We stayed with them for three nights. My room-mate for this stay was the wicket-keeper Rifaqat Ali. On the first night our hosts asked if we would like to play snooker with them. We had never seen the game before and could not quite understand how the big sticks could be used to hit the balls on a table, but I am keen to play every sport and I wanted to take them on. Rifaqat said, 'We do not know how to play this game', but I told him, 'If we just watch them for a while we can learn and then beat them.' It was not long before they said, 'Competition?' We both knew that word, along with 'win', 'lose' and a few others. At first we fouled, or missed the cue ball altogether. Then we hit on a plan and discussed it in our own language: I agreed to keep our opponents talking and to ask questions about the photos in the room and so on whilst Rifaqat cleared a few of the balls. I kept the brother and sister occupied looking at pictures, and soon all the balls were in the pockets. Rifaqat called out 'Look, we've won!' They said, 'How come we didn't hear the noise of the ball and stick?' We did not speak enough English to explain so we just jumped up and down crying, 'We beat Australia!' The next day we sat with the family and showed them with sign language how Rifaqat had pushed the balls into the pockets with his hands. I think they already knew, but we were all able to laugh about it.

I was still attempting to come to terms with the Western world when we went to the USA for a series of one-day promotional matches in 1989. My team-mate Aamir Malik asked me, the youngster, to get him a Big Mac from the McDonald's near our hotel. He gave me the money and told me to walk two streets to McDonald's and to ask for, 'Two Big Mac meals with strawberry milkshakes'. Rab Nawaz, the oldest umpire in domestic cricket, was with me when I left Aamir's room and he said, 'Look, I'll come with you and help you out.' He tried to make out that he knew what he was doing. As I made my way to the restaurant I kept repeating, 'Big Mac, Big Mac,' to help me remember what to order when I had to speak English. I also had to keep looking for the McDonald's sign so I knew which shop to go into. All of the English shop signs and advertisements, which were supposed to guide people, were simply confusing. You have to remember that all of the English letters meant little to me – I couldn't even sound out words very easily.

Rab and I walked into McDonald's and joined separate queues, but arrived at the counter at the about the same time. When the girl at the counter asked me for my order my mind went blank. There were queues behind us, the counter girl was talking really quickly and suddenly I felt the pressure of rising panic. I looked up, recognised the 'M' sign on the display, and remembered the word 'McDonald's'. So I asked for, 'Two McDonalds and a strawberry milkshake, please.' Rab, who did not really speak English either, heard what I said and ordered, 'One McDonalds and a strawberry milkshake.' The girls started laughing, presumably at the idea that we wanted to buy three restaurants between us. Other people in the queues found it amusing too and we became the centre of attention, much to Rab's discomfort. I was not too embarrassed but I thought, 'Something's going on here. I don't think I've said the right thing' After about 30 seconds the counter girl asked, 'Are you sure you need two McDonalds?' I said, 'Yes, please. Can I have two McDonalds?' She turned to her friend at Rab's till and started talking to her. I thought they were making jokes with each other, because they were both giggling, but the people behind were laughing too. I was keeping a straight face because I was trying to work out what was happening. However, Rab looked over and started to have serious words with me. He said 'Are you taking the mickey out of me? I'm an old man and I've come with you to keep you company. I don't think this is funny; you are making a fool out of me.' I tried to tell him that I did not know what was happening and we stood at the counter arguing to the amusement of everyone around. Some people tried to help us out by suggesting items from the menu but I couldn't understand them and I did not know what kind of burger to order. Eventually I looked at the board again and tried to remember my English letters from school. I saw 'B' – 'I' – 'G' and then the words came back to me – 'Big Mac!' At this point I was able to clarify my order: 'Sorry, sorry, excuse me. Big Mac, not McDonald's.' The girl laughed again, but produced the meals and I went back to the hotel to tell all the guys what had happened. I quite enjoyed the adventure because English was a strange language to me, but Rab was not happy at all. On the way to buy the burgers he had told me, 'I've been travelling the world for years.

English is no problem for me,' but he had still managed to get it all wrong.

The next day we were playing a charity match against India and when I came on to bowl the guys were all calling, 'C'mon now, let's get two McDonalds here' and things like that. They started to call me 'McDonald's' and Rab was getting angrier and angrier. I appealed for a leg before to Sanjay Manjrekar and he said, 'Not out! Just play the game and don't bother appealing to me.' Then he tossed me my cap in disgust. The players continued to wind him up. They told him that I had described the incident in McDonald's and he denied saying anything wrong. He said it was only me who made the mistake. For the rest of the match he never gave me a thing when I bowled from his end.

Although he helped me on occasions, Saeed Anwar would also make fun of me whenever he could. One of his favourite tricks was to call me on the telephone and put on a variety of English accents. He was always pretending to be someone else and I was never sure who I was talking to. Once I called his room to ask what we were going to do for dinner and he put on a voice denying that he was Saeed and asking me what I wanted and why I was calling. I tried ten times with the same response. I was so confused that I called the operator and asked to be put through to Mr Saeed Anwar in Room 230. When she put me through to his room he continued to pretend that it was not him. I was getting desperate so I called the hotel manager to ask if he had changed rooms. I was assured that he had not so eventually I realised what was happening and paid him a visit.

Telephones were used to play tricks on unpopular team managers. Our favourite trick was to use a lobby telephone to call reception and ask them to report to the manager that players were breaking the curfew and were in the bar. Someone would sneak out to do this at one or two o'clock in the morning. The manager would get out of bed and rush to the bar, but of course all the players were in their rooms. I remember one manager calling a meeting the next day and telling the team that he had firm evidence that players had broken the curfew, that he knew who they were and that they should come to him to confess in order to avoid serious punishment. We just kept our heads down and laughed to ourselves because he was never going to find out.

I know that this may sound like schoolboy stuff, but I honestly believe that some of the practical jokes helped to build team spirit and improve our performances. Team managers were always fair game and we would sometimes knock on their hotel room door and run away. After two or three knocks we knew that the manager would wait by the door to catch us, so we went back to bed. At breakfast we would laugh when the manager described the mysterious events of the night before.

I was still struggling with my command of the English language in 1993 when Somerset wanted me to play for them. So they spoke to Intikhab Alum, the tour manager at the time, and through him offered me a three-year contract, which I accepted. After agreeing terms with Somerset I was asked to do a short interview on television. I was sitting in a room with an earpiece in my ear and I heard the director say, 'The presenter will speak to you soon.' Almost immediately I heard, '1, 2, 3, action' but I did not realise that I was then live on air. The person in the studio was talking to me, but I had no one in front of me and was really unsure about what was happening. As I was confused I sat quietly, but I could hear the director repeating, 'Can you hear me?' I was looking around, thinking, 'Who's speaking?' Eventually I replied to the director that I could and asked if I should speak to the presenters or should I wait for them to come to me? They announced that there was a technical problem and that they would come back to the interview later. It was a real mess-up and my team-mates could not stop laughing when they saw me. In recent years I have been offered work with Sky Sports TV, but I do not think they would have been so quick to take me on had they seen my first efforts.

It was a strange experience for me off the pitch in Somerset because I was alone and experiencing a totally different lifestyle for the first time. In our culture you do not get together with your partner until you are married. So, although I was engaged to be married back in Pakistan, I was by myself in England. There were not many Asians in Somerset and although I had a couple of friends in London, it was difficult for them to come and see me on a regular basis. Looking back, this was a blessing in disguise because I was forced to throw myself in to English culture rather than just sit at home. My English improved dramatically – it had to, really, or I would not have had a life. Everyone spoke very slowly for me at first, but over the course of about two years, I became quite fluent and picked up the accents. I can even do a few impressions of people, including Sir Geoffrey Boycott, but you'll have to take my word for that.

I spent time with the players after games or on rest days. Seam bowler Neil Mallender looked after me particularly well; he spent a lot of time with me and showed me where to go and how to do things in England. He was a great help and he also helped me to drive in England during my second year. Driving was one area where I certainly needed help. It was a case of, 'Watch out drivers!' when Mushy was on the road. I think it may have been me who was the cause of road rage! Everywhere I went, people were blowing their horns, flashing their lights or sticking their fingers up at me. I would actually drive very quickly in Pakistan because that is the norm there, but I was so nervous in England that I would be one of the slowest drivers on the road. When driving in Pakistan you have to use full beam at night and it took me a while to adapt to the rules in England. As a result I used to drive in the middle of town with my full beam on and drivers coming the other way were constantly dazzled. I recall one occasion when a car turned round and followed me after I had been using my lights on full-beam. He was flashing his lights and blasting his horn at me, but I just carried on because I thought he wanted to kill me. I drove on for ages with him following me, and eventually stopped and told myself to be brave. The driver got out of his car and I braced myself for trouble, but he just said he wanted to help me and explained what I was doing wrong. I was a relieved man.

Once I gained confidence behind the wheel I began to drive a lot more aggressively, as I would in Pakistan. I was driving some of my team-mates through a winding country lane and overtook the car in front on a blind bend. They all ducked down and started shouting. They asked what I would have done if a car had been coming the other way. I told them drivers back home would not think twice about pulling off a manoeuvre like that; however, my passengers did not seem so keen and made me stop the car so someone else could drive.

My driving became quite legendary, especially after I had driven my sponsored car into the wall at the entrance to my driveway on three separate occasions. The club members all laughed and said, 'What do you expect, it is Mushy after all!' This hurt me and I told them it was not my fault. The driveway was too narrow and I had to drive into it quickly as it was on a busy road. Simon Ecclestone was not having any of that, and he came round to show me how to park the car. He showed me just perfectly by putting a big scratch down the side!

As an easy-going guy, I was often involved in practical jokes. In Australia in 1995 Inzamam, my room-mate, was due to bat the following day and had gone to bed early. I went out for dinner with Wasim and a few others and did not get back until about midnight. I did not want to disturb Inzi so I opened the door quietly and heard him wheezing and breathing a little more noisily than he usually did when he slept. I quietly asked, 'Inzi? Inzi?' and he stopped making the noise. I sat on my bed, took my shoes off and was facing the door of the room when suddenly someone jumped on me shouting, 'Oooh, aagh!' I hit him with my elbow, but he was far too big to fight off. The attack went on for about 30 seconds and at first I thought there was someone else in the room. Once I realised it was Inzi I said, 'This isn't funny! I could have had a heart attack!' I was really shocked. He thought the whole thing was hilarious and could not wait to tell the team the next day. They, of course, took the mickey out of me about it whenever they could.

Wasim, Waqar, Aaqib Javed and I were great friends in 1992 and we spent a lot of time together. One day on the England tour Wasim and Waqar decided to collect all the bottles of aftershave and perfume they could find. Then they went into the room I was sharing with Aaqib and emptied every bottle into our beds, on our pillows, in the bathrooms and anywhere else they could. When Aaqib and I left the lift I said, 'Aaqib, it smells very nice up here. I think the posh ladies are staying on our floor.' We had to walk quite a way to our room and as we got closer the smell was getting stronger and stronger. I said, 'I think a Royal family or someone from Hollywood is here. We need to keep our eyes open to see who they are.' When we opened the door to our room we were completely overwhelmed by the smell. We were only in the room for about five minutes before we had to go to the physio to ask for some Panadols. Our headaches were terrible. We could not sleep in the room so we went to the manager. We knew that it must be someone from the team, but no one would let on. Wasim and Waqar kept very quiet, as we were getting more and more annoyed. We told everyone that we would be having a very serious talk with the people concerned when we found out who it was.

In those days we were very relaxed in practice and would play fielding games where you had to spin around a few times and then catch a ball that was thrown to you. Aaqib and I were nowhere near the ball the next day. We still had bad headaches and were really out of sorts. The headaches stayed for two days, but we could not be angry for long as it was such a funny trick.

A relaxed approach sometimes helped when the dressing-room was tense. I remember a time at Headingley in 1996 when Wasim, batsman Ijaz Ahmed, and I were sitting in the bathing area trying to relax during a match. Ijaz was next man in and he sat in an empty bathtub with his kit on and his legs dangling over each side. Wasim quietly reached behind Ijaz and turned on the cold shower, which erupted over him. He leapt up screaming and the management ran in to see what was happening, but whilst Ijaz was angry about being soaked it took his mind off the pressure of waiting to bat. He went on to make a fifty, so the cold water treatment must have worked.

Learning the language has been a long process, but it has increased the pressure on me when I play cricket. When I first began to play international cricket I would hear the Australians shouting to each other as I was batting, but had no idea what they were saying. After I learned English I realised that they were encouraging the fast bowlers to hit me with bouncers to try and break my fingers. Had I known, I would have been far more frightened than I was, but maybe not as scared as I was in our own dressing-room in 1992.

Intikhab Alam, the tour manager, always followed a set routine when he showered and dressed. First he would put on his shirt, then his underpants and finally his trousers. After play during a tour match at Northants he showered and came out wearing his shirt and a towel around his waist. I was sitting next to his spot in the corner and I could see that he was looking around for about five minutes. Then he shouted, 'Whoever has made this joke is going to have a serious problem.' I did not understand what he was talking about so I said, 'What happened, Skip?' He said, 'Somebody has nicked my underpants.' Now, he was a highly respected senior person who had captained Pakistan, so this surprised me. I said, 'Skip, they must be somewhere here.' He said, 'No, I've looked everywhere and someone has obviously made a joke, but I'll be very angry with them when I find out who it is.' I thought this would have serious consequences, because we did not play tricks on the senior people like this. Someone said to him, 'Skip, why don't you look in the bags. Maybe someone is trying to steal your underpants and has put them in his bag.' So I thought, 'Yes, why not. This seems a good idea.' They looked in every bag except mine and his pants were not found. Javed Miandad, the captain, said, 'Sorry Skip, it must be someone from outside the dressing-room who has come in to take them. We've checked every bag . . . oh, except Mushy's, but he wouldn't have them.' Then he looked at me and said, 'Mushy, do you have Skip's underwear?' Remember, this was the captain asking and the most senior player was getting angrier and angrier. I said, 'No, of course not. You can look in my bag.' As I said this I opened my bag and the first thing I saw was Skip's underwear.

The colour drained from my face immediately. I went yellow and started to panic. Intikhab stared straight into my eyes and said, 'Why did you do that?' I stammered, 'Skip, I promise, I swear to God, I did not put them in my bag. I don't know how they got there.' For a while I wondered what was going to happen to me. I thought maybe they would send me back from the tour. After about five minutes I saw Javed break into a big laugh because he was the one who had set up the joke. In fact he was the only man in the dressing-room who could have played a joke on Intikhab. To this day people still laugh about the time I tried to nick Skipper's underwear.

5

My Country, My Captains I:
The Early Years

'There are plenty of people who are not big occasion players. Why? Because nobody tells them "I will back you up and support you. You do your best and I will not drop you."'

After the Youth World Cup, I returned home to play for United Bank but it was while playing for Pakistan Under-19s against India Under-19s that I caught the eye of someone who would have an extraordinary impact on my life. The Under-19s were to play a four-match series against India, who were a strong side with players such as Nayyan Mongia, Ajay Jadeja and Aashish Kapoor beginning to make an impact. I think the original idea was for each player to feature in two Tests so that the selectors could have a look at us all. However, my performances kept me in the side for all four matches and by the end of the series I had a really high profile. The First Test was televised and I scored a quick-fire fifty in addition to taking two or three wickets. The Second Test went even better for me as I scored 65 and took twelve wickets during the match. I finished as the highest wicket-taker with over 30 wickets and scored three fifties in the four-Test series. Fortunately, Imran Khan had seen at least one of the Test matches and he decided that he needed this young all-rounder for the next international tournament in Sharjah.

Imran Khan (1989–1992)
Imran Khan was a great leader and he preferred to pick players who he could see had big match temperament, rather than those who just

looked to have good technique in the nets. He had a great eye for picking players and was honest and brave in his decision-making. He was an achiever and his decisions were right almost all of the time. I'm not sure if the selectors would have considered me, but Imran was a great captain with huge influence and he said that he wanted me in the squad, so I was selected. Imran was the only captain I knew who was able to make all selection decisions on his own – he even stopped selectors from coming to see people in the practice camp if he did not want them there.

The squad of fourteen had to attend a pre-tour training camp, but I did not meet Imran there as he was in England. I first met him on the coach as we were leaving the hotel in Sharjah. He was the last to board the coach and everyone, the coaches and the senior players, had left the single seat at the front empty. It was clearly left for Imran, who sat on it with great confidence. This was the first time I had ever seen my role-model in the flesh and after about five minutes of looking at him in awe I said 'Hello.' As I did, I lowered my face and turned my eyes to the ground, because I could not believe that I was so close to him and did not feel able to look him in the eyes when he replied.

We had fielding practice at the ground and I noticed Imran watching me, and I must say I was pretty quick in the field in those days. We then had a net and he saw me bowling and batting. The next day, before the match started, somebody told me that I was the focus of a big article that morning in the *Khaleej Times*. I could not read English, so a liaison officer brought the paper to my room and read it to me. In the article, Imran said that I had a good future, that I had the temperament needed and with my enthusiasm, energy and talent he expected great things of me. Even before I had left my room I felt like I had taken five wickets!

On March 23 1989 I made my one-day debut against Sri Lanka. The match did not start very well for me as I was caught behind off Ravi Ratnayeke for a duck. It was very disappointing because Imran had told people that I could bat and put a lot of faith in me. Thankfully, things were completely different in the field. I caught the Sri Lankan opener Roshan Mahanama with a smart catch at midwicket and I could see from Imran's response that he was delighted, not just because we had taken a wicket, but for me that I had made a good start and for the team because his decision to select me was paying off. I then bowled a very good spell of 9.3-1-33-2, including the prize scalp of Aravinda de Silva. I was really excited and confident from the start of the innings to the finish and Imran had a lot to do with that. Before I bowled he came to me and said, 'Just go and bowl and tell me what field you want.' I thought, 'Imran Khan is asking ME what field I want. Here I am, a youngster of eighteen, and the mighty Imran Khan is asking me to set the field.' The way in which he spoke to me and his body language told me that he was very positive. He inspired me to be positive, and I was so pleased to be involved that I did not get nervous. I did not even realise I had got out de Silva. Afterwards, no one could keep me quiet. I was like an actor on the big stage trying to impress everyone. However, after the game, Imran again stated he was convinced I had the right temperament to play Test cricket and that I was a good team player. I felt increasingly confident about my game and myself. This was a feature of Imran's captaincy. He rarely said much to you in person, but he would praise you in TV and newspaper interviews.

My selection for Pakistan enabled me to meet my future wife, Uzma, in 1989. I was with the squad in the Intercontinental Hotel, Lahore when her brother sent her over to get some autographs from the famous players. She did not ask for mine, but as soon as I saw her eyes (yes, I know – but it's true!) I knew that she was the one for me. I 'forced' my autograph on her and then courted her through her brother by getting tickets for matches that they could both attend. We were engaged in 1992 and married in 1994.

By the time of the 1991 Wills Trophy series in Sharjah I found it a little easier to speak to Imran. We were facing the West Indies when Viv Richards came in to bat on a very flat wicket. Neither fast bowlers nor spinners had a chance to stop anybody making big runs. So here was the King of cricket walking to the crease and I was the bowler. Imran came to me and said, 'What field do you want?' I said, 'I want a short silly point.' To be honest, even in a four-day match you would not put a man there to Viv, so this was a very unusual request in a one-day match. I also said, 'I need mid-on and mid-off up and let's see what happens.' Imran asked me to justify the field, and I said, 'Skipper, if his ego gets hurt, he might make a mistake and maybe we can pick up his wicket.' I could tell from Imran's eyes that he was delighted I thought that the King could make mistakes. He loved the idea and said, 'Absolutely brilliant! Go for it!'

The players were in position and Rameez Raja appealed for a bat–pad catch off the first ball. The next three went for boundaries. Viv smashed me everywhere, but Imran came to me and said, 'This is brilliant. This attitude will make you a great cricketer and I don't care if you go for a hundred runs in ten overs. I need you to act like that all the time.'

After that tour, we went to the USA to play some exhibition matches against India. We played at the baseball stadium in New York and Sunil Gavaskar kept blasting the ball at me at point. I was stopping everything – I felt like I was covering all the ground from short third man to the covers. Imran never stopped smiling. I could see he was really happy with me; he did not need to say it because I could feel it. From then on, whenever he had a chance, he would talk about me. In fact, I was never dropped from a squad while Imran was in charge. Quite often, Abdul Qadir would get the nod over me for the final XI and, to be honest, I was not good enough to compete with him at the time. I was not even thinking about competing; I was there to learn. I used to watch everything Imran and Abdul did: I studied their movements, behaviour, how they batted, bowled, fielded, and even how they ate and dressed. I would copy everything.

The positive attitude that Imran helped instil in players went a long way in setting the foundations for our future success. Early in my one-day career, Australia hammered 300 against us in a miserable defeat at Brisbane in 1990. Tom Moody opened and smashed 89 and, although I eventually got him and Steve Waugh out, I bowled my ten overs for 76 and I thought it was bad news. I was happy enough with my performance and told a couple of the senior players as we left the field that I did not feel I had bowled too badly. They just laughed at me and told me to check my figures, and deep down I was worrying what the selectors would make of my expensive spell. During the lunch break we were sitting eating in the dining-room when I felt a hand on my shoulder. I looked back and saw Imran standing over me. He had great charisma and everyone was paying attention when he said, 'You bowled absolutely brilliantly,' in front of everyone. And then he walked away. I was amazed, but delighted.

Later, my confidence was boosted once more when he took me aside to tell me that on another day I could easily have got five for 30. I suppose he was trying to build my confidence for the next game; if he was, then it certainly worked. We went on to play in Sydney, where we scraped home by 2 runs. I scored a run-a-ball unbeaten 17 in the first innings, which proved to be quite vital, then took two for 46 off my ten overs, including the wicket of Steve Waugh again. Leg-spinners may not bowl too well one day, but they can win the next game all on their own. A great captain like Imran Khan recognises this and keeps their confidence up on the bad days. This often pays off, because I believe a top quality leg-spinner can win two games out of five. If you do not believe me, look at Shane Warne!

Back home in Pakistan, my captains were not as positive. United Bank would drop me every second game. They would always pick other spinners for the high-profile games on TV. The press were often critical of my selection for the national team and would openly ask how Mushtaq Ahmed could be picked for Pakistan when he could not get into the United Bank team. One day, after a practice session at a camp in Lahore, Imran came to me and said, 'Mushtaq, while I am captain no one will be able to touch you. Don't worry about selection, because you will be involved in every tour and every game while I am captain. Now, ignore what they are saying and go out and build your reputation on the field.' I just thought, 'Well, that's it. That's all I need to hear. I can concentrate on playing and I don't need to worry about tomorrow.' My captain was offering the same advice and example that I received from my father, and it filled me with confidence and the positive spirit that I needed to succeed.

Imran was a very private person. We would rarely see him after a game as he would not interfere with our dining arrangements and would not invite others to dine with him. On the odd occasion, once I was established, he invited Wasim Akram, Aaqib Javed, Waqar Younis, Ijaz Ahmed and me to join him for dinner, but he really kept himself to himself most of the time. It was his charisma and character that made him a celebrity. On the plane to America I recall some ladies asking who we were, as we were all in our team uniforms. They had no idea about cricket, but we explained that we were the Pakistan cricket team. Their immediate reaction was to ask, 'Is Imran Khan here, on the plane?' They were very excited and insisted on going to see him.

Imran always believed that he was the best fielder, batsman and bowler in the team and was the match-winner, but he was also a humble man in many ways. In 1989, my first year in the Test squad, I was throwing the ball down to him in the nets as he practised his pull shot. After feeding him for thirty minutes he was not getting consistent success and I said, 'You're not doing this very well.' Now, this was a dangerous thing to say. Who would tell the great Imran Khan that he was not playing correctly? It should not have been me on my first tour! However, when the ball was at eye level he was sometimes edging it or missing it so it hit him on the head. I felt that I had to tell him what I thought. Thankfully he said, 'What should I do?' I told him, 'Don't close your eyes. Keep them open and watch the ball until you hit it.' He said, 'That's a very good point. Why don't you bowl me with a tennis ball so I can get this right?' I was almost fainting with fatigue as he kept me in the nets for another hour or more while he perfected his technique.

Imran's huge self-belief crossed over into every aspect of his public life and helped to make him famous beyond cricket. His cricketing legacy was a winning team for Pakistan. Once he took over we started winning everything from Test matches to the World Cup. He picked players who wanted to play, rather than those with reputations or talent but who lacked the big match temperament or the hunger to win. He instilled in us the belief that if we did not let ourselves down, we would not let the people down. With players who were not frightened of failure, we were destined to succeed.

Javed Miandad (1992–1993)

Before I first came to England to play Test cricket, I had heard people say that the English climate and pitches were very different and that it was not a place for spinners as the conditions offered no help. I did not believe it – I always thought if you were good enough, there was no reason to think like that. My attitude when we toured England in 1992 was that I had been blessed with talent and I could play anywhere. I played every game of that tour and took 68 wickets, including five in Test matches. In fact I had played in England already and knew that I could take wickets.

My first trip to England came back in 1990, when I stayed with Waqar Younis for two months and watched him play for Surrey. During this time Massoud Anwar, a left-arm spinner who played with me at United Bank, called to offer me some games with Darlington as he was injured. The chairman, Brian Dobson, offered me £150 a game and I played six matches, taking over 40 wickets. After my final game Mr Dobson gave me an extra £200 and thanked me for my commitment and performances. Whenever I go to Chester-le-Street to play Durham he comes to see me, and I have very fond memories of those few games.

The Pakistan board decided to bring Javed Miandad back as captain for the England tour of 1992. He was very experienced, having captained the team on many occasions between 1979 and 1991. In contrast, this was going to be my first-class debut in England and I was really looking forward to it. We had already proved ourselves as a one-day side, but we were determined to show our worth in the Test arena because some critics doubted our ability in the longer form of the game. We had the added incentive of the Tetley Bitter Challenge, in which we had to beat ten out of thirteen first-class counties to win a bonus of £100,000.

Javed was a superb cricketer and a great man. He was undoubtedly one of the finest batsmen that Pakistan ever produced, but I did not get the same enjoyment from playing under him as a captain as I had during Imran's reign. His approach with players was to tell them straight out if he felt they were not good enough. If I had a bad bowling spell, his reaction would be to tell me, 'That's it for you. You won't stay in my squad, bowling like that.' Where Imran would come down to your level when speaking to you to make you feel comfortable, Javed expected you to go to him and live up to his expectations in order to be respected. In my view, if you want to get a good performance from your team you have to win the players' hearts. I believe that a good leader is more like a servant who finds the best way to deal with each person in the house. Javed never really succeeded in this. He always wanted to continue the conversations about cricket throughout the evening after a hard day in the field when we were tired and just wanted to relax. I was frightened to be on his table at dinner because I knew he would bombard me with questions about what I had done wrong on the pitch during the day. He was never satisfied with a batsman when he failed to score a hundred, but if everyone scored a hundred we would have a total of over 1,000, which is not going to happen. Similarly, every bowler cannot take five wickets in an innings. We have to accept that some people have their day and others do not. When you are constantly reminded that you have had a bad day and asked to analyse it all evening, you begin to get nervous about playing the next day. It is not fair to compare captains, but I think that Javed felt that he needed to control everything and if he did not he would lose respect, whereas Imran was so sure of himself that he was comfortable when other players did their own thing.

As it happened, the 1992 tour proved to be my best tour of England, although they had quality players like Graham Gooch, Alec Stewart, Graeme Hick, Robin Smith, Allan Lamb, Ian Botham and David Gower in the team. We lost the first game of our Tetley Bitter Challenge against Worcestershire, but went on to win the remaining games and collect the prize. However, we did poorly in the one-day games, losing 4-1. The Test series would prove to be more successful. We got a draw out of the first match at Edgbaston, and then it was on to Lord's.

As the senior players reminded us, Lord's was the home of cricket and a very special ground. This was my first trip to HQ, and after the first practice session I lay on the turf and looked around me thinking, 'How lucky am I? The greatest cricketers in the world have played on this pitch, and now I have my chance to play here, too.' I ran my fingers through the grass, which felt more like a carpet, and thought back to the conditions that I had endured only a few years before, chasing the ball amongst the stones and rubbish in railway stations and sidings.

The match was one of the best I ever played in. We took a series lead with a tense two-wicket win and I took two wickets in the first innings; in the second I bowled nine overs for 32 runs and took the wickets of Graeme Hick, Robin Smith and Allan Lamb before lunch. I also had Ian Botham dropped behind. I hardly ate a thing during the break and was so excited because I thought that I was on for a five-wicket haul. I could almost see my name written up on the board in the visitors' dressing-room which records the great performances. We had a team meeting and Javed said, 'Don't take anything for granted here. We need to bowl them out and every run is very important, so keep it tight. We are going to start as we finished, so Mushy, you will be at the Nursery End. Waqar, continue from the Pavilion.' But as we went down from the dressing-room I heard Wasim talking to Javed. He said, 'The ball is reverse swinging. If Waqar and I start, maybe we can get through them quicker. Mushy may do it, but could go for a few runs.' Javed said, 'No, he just took three wickets; we should give him a chance,' but Wasim insisted that the ball would reverse swing. Javed still said that I would bowl, so I felt good as we took to the field. My logic told me that if Waqar tired, Wasim could take over from him and I could keep bowling from my end. Then, as I was stretching before going to my mark, Javed came over and said, 'Have a rest. Wasim is starting.' I was very disappointed, but said nothing as I understood that Wasim's idea did make sense. I also respect him for having such strong belief in his own ability, even though he did not have so much confidence in mine.

In around ten overs Wasim took four wickets and Waqar took a couple to finish England off. We were set a target of just 138 to win, but collapsed to 95 for eight before Wasim and Waqar guided us home. They had already put us on top with two great bowling performances and they should not have had to make the runs as well.

We actually felt that we had thrown the game and the dressing-room was very tense as they brought us victory and established a series lead. Pakistani batsmen always had problems playing in England. We would struggle against the swinging ball and often nick it to the slips. However, on this occasion we came out on top.

We drew the Third Test at Old Trafford and then lost the Fourth at Headingley, but we captured the series at the Oval in the Fifth and final Test, where we won by ten wickets. In almost Asian conditions, our bowlers were able to enjoy a lot of reverse swing. Wasim and Waqar were young and hungry and were on the top of their game during that tour; Aaqib Javed completed an excellent pace trio.

The whole tour was a great experience, with a lot of players on top form. From the moment we arrived at Heathrow we were greeted by hundreds of Pakistani fans, who chanted our names and hailed us as heroes for having won the World Cup. This kind of treatment became the norm around the country. Restaurants filled with well-wishers and autograph hunters whenever we were there, and the support in the grounds boosted the team throughout the series. Even English fans queued outside our hotels to ask for autographs whenever we left the building. For a young lad like me it was a whole new experience and I loved every moment, especially as we seemed be winning all the time. It also helped that the senior players were not around a lot of the time, which meant we could have some fun because we had to be quiet when they were around. It was my most enjoyable tour, and the only downside was that Imran was not there with us.

Unfortunately, a series of memorable performances was clouded with money issues. Having completed the Tetley Bitter Challenge and earned the £100,000 bonus, the senior players such as Javed, Wasim, Salim Malik and Rameez Raja introduced a 'Celeb System' for sharing out the money. This meant that the players with most caps took the lion's share, leaving the younger players with less of the pot. It was a kick in the teeth for the newcomers in the side, particularly as they had played the majority of the games and the split of the money had not been announced until we had won the prize money. Moin Khan, Waqar, Aaqib and I went to Javed and said, 'Look, this isn't fair. Why has this "Celeb System" been introduced? We've never seen it on a tour before. We should get equal money.' Javed was not happy at all. He said 'Why are you always thinking about money instead of playing cricket? You have only just started playing for Pakistan and you are becoming greedy.' We felt that we had made our point and we left his room having accepted the decision, but we realised it was one-way with Javed and it was disappointing because we felt we deserved more respect from the senior players. Javed thought about himself first and foremost; he was a totally different man to Imran, who would try to get the same things for all the players.

The start of the 'Celeb System' was the beginning of a difficult period in Pakistan cricket. Although we were winning, the atmosphere in the dressing-room changed and, as you will see in later chapters, the younger players went back to concentrating on making their own reputations. A climate had been established which would lead to serious problems when the team was not performing so well.

Javed's approach to captaincy can be summed up by an incident in Hamilton, New Zealand in 1993. I think it was his last Test as captain. I had taken two wickets in the first innings, and went on to take three for 87, but as we came in for lunch Javed said to me, 'Don't take lunch. Go into the nets and bowl.' Now, if I had decided that I needed to do this because I was not feeling right, I would have asked him if I could. But I felt that I was doing OK and I needed a rest and time to reflect on my performance. I did as I was told because I have been brought up to respect my seniors, but it left me feeling very negative.

6

My Country, My Captains II Dressing-room Rebellion

'Every Pakistan captain plays in the shadow of Imran Khan'

Wasim Akram (1992–94, 1995–99)

During 1992/93 the dressing-room was very unsettled. We played a one-day triangular series in Australia against West Indies and the hosts. It was at this time that we started to lose everything. We were not performing well as a team and relationships within the squad began to suffer as individuals began to look for other people to blame. Wasim was ready to take over from Javed and the board, unhappy with Javed's captaincy, decided he had to make way for a younger man. They dropped Javed as captain but retained him as a player. Wasim Akram was appointed, with Waqar Younis as vice-captain, for the 1992/93 tour of West Indies.

Wasim and Waqar had been winning matches for Pakistan and we started beautifully under Wasim's captaincy. We began with the Wills Trophy in Sharjah, where we beat Zimbabwe and Sri Lanka and then Sri Lanka again in the final. From there we went to South Africa for a one-day series. We beat South Africa twice, but lost the final to the West Indies. However, we felt that we were playing well and that everyone in the camp was pulling in the same direction.

Unfortunately, when we went to the West Indies at the start of 1993 things began to drift again. The tour proved to be a nightmare, with a serious incident occurring in Grenada which I describe elsewhere. It was my most difficult tour, even though in Wasim and

Waqar we had a very, very good partnership in the team – the best I have ever seen – and Wasim was a great cricketer and a very lovely man. I feel honoured to have had a friend like him. He has a great sense of humour and makes everyone laugh. Waqar, Wasim, Aaqib and I spent a lot of time together as we were all of a similar age. He was also a terrific role model as a player. However, when we began to play under his captaincy he tried to act like Imran Khan. He was not naturally like Imran and was not able to carry this off. For example, when Imran would criticise someone in the field – maybe shout at them if he felt they were scared of the ball or not pulling their weight – we knew that Imran was doing this for love. There was always love behind the criticism. When Wasim did the same thing, there was not any love behind it. He was rude and critical of players in the field, even if they were giving him everything they had. Imran could be as critical as Wasim, but a lot of the players were the same age as Wasim, or older, and his approach did not work. Many players were upset by his approach and team morale was very bad as we went on to lose the three-match series 2-0.

It was a shame, because off the pitch Wasim was fine. He had a friendly nature, but he felt that to be our leader he needed to be a hard man. He was very aggressive and would swear at a fielder who dropped a catch, even though no one would do so deliberately. Sometimes, when the opposition were playing well with a good partnership developing, Wasim would lose his mind. He was not helping us, himself or his captaincy. At the time we thought he was a bit over-the-top and that we were not *that* bad and did not deserve to be treated that way. He did not understand the art of man-management or appreciate that you can get results by speaking softly. I think a good captain needs to be a good listener so people will even go to him with personal problems, but Wasim felt the tough approach would gain him respect. He was wrong.

We played the Pepsi Champions Trophy series in Sharjah in November 1993, during which Wasim broke his arm. Although he was officially captain for the Zimbabwe Tests in Pakistan in December 1993 Waqar was captain on the field. Following this series the players decided not to play under Wasim's captaincy.

There was no single incident; we simply felt that as Pakistan cricketers we should be treated more courteously. Nine players, including myself, spoke out against him in January 1994. The Pakistani media made a big issue of this, which forced a meeting of all concerned with the Pakistan Cricket Board (PCB) at the Lahore Cricket Ground. The chairman of the board was Javed Bakir. The president of Pakistan and the PCB, Farooq Leghari, was also at the meeting alongside Arafa Batchi, a Board member from Karachi. Javed was a cousin of Imran and a big personality in Pakistan politics. When we arrived at the meeting, the first thing Javed Bakir said was, 'Are you sure you are not going to play under his captaincy? You do know the consequences there will be for you guys?' We said, 'Yes, we all know that, but we are not going to change our minds.' At the meeting, they asked me first of all what the problem was with Wasim's captaincy. He was actually sitting next to me, so it was obviously an uncomfortable moment. I replied that he was my friend and always will be, but they said, 'How can you do this and be his friend?' I said, 'This is a different issue, as I am not enjoying my cricket under his captaincy.'

Everyone at the table gave his opinion, but the meeting did not work in our favour. Two days later we were summoned to a meeting in the Pearl Continental Hotel, Lahore, where the president told us that the PCB had decided to ban all nine players for two years from all first-class cricket and to stop our salaries from our employers. Naturally, it was a very worrying time. A few of the players weakened and asked how they were going to feed their families, but we stuck together and said our unity would prevail if we stayed strong together. The PCB threatened us by announcing a new side made up of youngsters with Wasim as captain and reasserted that this was our last chance to change our minds and save our careers. One of us – it may have been Waqar, maybe one of the others – said, 'Sir, if you say to us, "jump from this window" we will respect you for that and jump for nothing, but we are not going to change our decision. We are nine players and we know this is it, but we are willing to face the consequences.'

They told us that they would talk to us again in one hour, but we were left in little doubt that we were facing a bleak future. After the hour we met again and we all thought we would be given our letters confirming our ban, but amazingly they said Wasim was no longer captain. Waqar was playing brilliantly and they knew that he wanted to take over from Wasim, but they said that they were not prepared to make him captain. Instead they chose Salim Malik, who had been dropped much earlier so was not even in the squad. He was made captain from nowhere, which was not popular with some of the senior players. The PCB also made Majid Khan the team manager, which was a good decision because he had a very strong personality and would put a stop to the in-fighting. Wasim would not speak to us for three or four weeks. He bowled brilliantly on the New Zealand tour following his sacking, but relations between him and the rest of the team were very strained. He stopped speaking to us: I remember he and his wife were coming out of the lift to go for dinner and I greeted him, 'Salaam ala quum,' but he just smiled and did not say anything. I went to my room and reflected on the events leading up to that moment. However, we know that time is the biggest healer and after a while we were OK.

Things slowly improved and we tried to talk to him and welcome him back as a player. He began to talk again and accepted the situation. We became friends again and I still hold Wasim in high esteem. I was the focus of his anger at first because he felt I was the ringleader, but I personally stick by our actions because I think it benefited Pakistani cricket. Wasim and I discussed the incident a while later and he maintained that we had been in the wrong. I told him to leave it in the past, and said that it would not do any good to discuss it further. If you continue to think about times like that you will be after revenge, which will be no good for you or anybody.

Looking back, I can now see that we were wrong to have acted without first talking to him about our concerns. The problem was that we were very young at the time. The senior players who were around us were very clever. They thought, 'Why should we get involved in this conflict?' They knew that they could get youngsters such as Waqar, Inzi, Moin Khan, Rashid Latif and me to take responsibility for any problems that were caused. They saw us as aggressive people who were trying to make names for ourselves, and they used to motivate us against Wasim. They would play us off against Wasim saying, 'Don't fight with him, but we heard that he was saying something against you. Maybe you aren't playing tomorrow. Don't mention my name, but I want you to know because you're a lovely man, but don't fight against him . . .' They sowed the seeds of doubt and we were not mature enough to deal with the situation. So we made a big mistake. The night before we went to the Board we had dinner with Wasim at his house and never said a word about our intentions. In hindsight we should have said, 'Wasim, we're not happy. Please sort out your captaincy and thinking or we will have to take this action.' That would have been the right thing to do, but we did not say anything to him that night. We had mentioned it to him a couple of times during matches, telling him that we did not think he should have acted as he did, but he always said, 'Look, I don't do it from my heart – it's just a heat of the moment thing.' So we let it run until we finally took our concerns to the PCB.

There was a little postscript to these events, but it happened on the county circuit the following summer. Wasim was a great cricketer, a fiercely fast bowler and a legend, and he was very angry with me because I was one of the nine. Somerset were playing Lancashire, and he bowled a long spell in which he took lots of wickets. He was resting in the field when I came into bat but I saw him go to his captain and I knew he was asking to have another bowl – at me! A left-arm spinner was bowling from the other end and I just closed my eyes to him and swung the bat, hoping to get out because I did not want to face Wasim. Well, everything came off the middle of the bat. The spinner put a man back and tried everything, but I kept hitting him over the top, and finding gaps to the boundaries to score 38 or 40 in two or three overs. Eventually I had to face Wasim and his first ball was a bouncer. I thought that I was going to get hit so I decided to take the challenge, watch the ball and be brave. I finally top-edged a catch off the bowling of Mike Watkinson.

When Wasim became captain again in 1995 he was a changed

man and one of the best captains I've ever played under after Imran. I'm delighted to say that by the time he was reappointed we were firm friends again. He was both brilliant tactically and with the players; he had learned from his mistakes and knew that he had to take the players with him. I was not picked for the First Test in Brisbane and Shane Warne took eleven wickets, but the Australian press have to take some of the credit for their success. The media in Australia are very clever and they had a big influence on our team selection. How so? Well, I had been bowling very well on the tour, taking many wickets in the three-day matches. At the other end was Saqlain Mushtaq. He would go on to be a great spin bowler for Pakistan, but at the time he was less experienced and I think that the Australians thought that they could get the better of him. So the press talked about him all the time, telling the world that he had a great mystery ball, the doosra, and the cameras were on him every moment that he was stretching, bowling in the nets and so on. At the same time they ignored me. I do not mean to be proud, but I think that this influenced our selectors who picked Saqlain ahead of me for the First Test in Brisbane. He took two wickets for 130 in the first innings, and McGrath had him lbw for 0 in the first innings. The Aussies forced us to follow on and beat us by an innings and 126 runs with Saqlain finishing on 2 not out. As a result I was back in contention for the next match.

I played in the Second Test in Hobart, and this was vital for my career. I took nine wickets (five and four) in the game and people started to compare Warney and me. I took a further nine wickets in the Third Test in Sydney. This was the first time Pakistan had won in Sydney and the press took a great deal of interest in me. I was honoured that Mark Taylor described me as the most difficult leg-spinner he had ever played against. Brian Lara also honoured me in much the same way, with both men remarking on the range of variation I employed.

I had just taken eighteen wickets in two Test matches in Australia, but when we arrived in Christchurch, New Zealand the wicket was green. A meeting took place with the captain and some senior players, and I was sure we were going to go for four fast bowlers. The batsmen were in favour of fast bowlers and I thought it made sense. When we arrived at the ground on the day of the match the wicket had been cut shorter and the debate started again. After considering all the options, the likelihood of the pitch flattening, fast bowlers getting tired or injured and so on it was finally decided that I would play. I took three for 115 and seven for 56 proving to myself once more that if you face your obstacles – in this case a green-top wicket – and give your best, Allah will sometimes take care of you.

In 1996 we toured England and for the first time in history the captains, Michael Atherton and Wasim Akram, tossed to select the type of ball we would use. One was a 'Duke', the other a 'Reader'. They thought that the 'Reader' would reverse swing more. If Atherton won the toss he would go for a 'Duke'. Wasim would always select the 'Reader'. I remember playing for Pakistan against my own team, Somerset, and taking ten wickets. As a result they offered me another two-year contract, which I was delighted with. I was able to visit Lord's once more with my national team. In 1992 I was close to achieving a 'five-for' under Javed Miandad. On this occasion, four years later, I took five for 57 in the second innings to realise my dream of having my name on the board in the visitors' dressing-room. The achievement came late in my career, but I was patient and received my reward for being honest with myself. As you will read later, I had experienced some dark hours during the previous two years. My career had been dogged by injury and life in Somerset had begun to change me as a person, but I had worked hard and placed my faith in Allah. As a result I was relaxed and did not even think about how many wickets I might take in the match.

We had thought the Lord's Test was heading for a draw. On the fourth evening we gave England a bat and Atherton and Alec Stewart started very well. At the close they were 89 for one. The next day rain was forecast after lunch, and we were really just playing out time. England were chasing 400 in bright sunshine, but we did not think they would have time to get them. I asked Wasim, 'Should I try going around the wicket?' He said, 'Fine, just bowl a couple of overs and we'll bring on some non-specialist bowlers to give ourselves some rest ahead of the coming Test matches.' I came on from the

Nursery End and bowled the entire session as England began the chase. I did not get any success and they raced to 189 for one. However, after lunch I took five wickets in 36 balls. Stewart, Atherton, Graeme Thorpe, Mark Ealham and Alan Mullally all fell, bang, bang, bang, in no time. Five minutes after we had taken England's last wicket the heavens opened, and we celebrated our victory in the rain. Waqar took four wickets in each innings and bowled the longest spell of his life to try and take a fifth, but could not do it. Wasim came on and took the final wicket with his first ball.

After the game, someone from the TV company came to me and said, 'Mushtaq, you're Man of the Match. Can you be ready in five minutes and we'll take you down for interviews and presentations.' I changed quickly and put on my Pakistan shirt and my lion's claw chain, washed my face, smoothed my hair and came out of the washroom to the dressing-room to be told, 'Sorry, mate, it's very poor form, but the decision has been changed and Waqar is now Man of the Match.' I groaned, 'Oh, no . . .' but then I had to laugh. I was delighted with my five wickets and pleased for Waqar.

Moin Khan came into the side at Headingley and scored a hundred in a drawn game. The final game was at the Oval and the Creator blessed me with two wickets in the first innings and the first six wickets of the second innings for 78 runs. I was awarded Man of the Match and Man of the Series. The two trophies were an honour for me, but we should not forget that it was under Wasim Akram that Pakistan began winning again and began to show the form that we had developed under Imran. Wasim had become a great captain.

I was struggling with an injury to my right knee throughout the England tour. The doctor gave me regular cortisone injections, but by the time we went to Toronto in September 1996 for the Sahara Cup it was very painful. We played India, against whom you must play very hard. The series was tied at 2-2 and the fifth match would decide the cup. After the fourth game I could not move my leg and it was very sore. The team management took me to a Canadian doctor, who knew nothing about cricket but had enough experience of ice hockey to recognise the symptoms I described. They diagnosed that my knee was very rough inside and that I needed arthroscopy. The PCB said that I could stay on for the operation after the final match. Allah gave me another lucky day and I took five for 36 and gained the Man of the Match award against India. This was a great honour. I enjoyed the day because I am very conscious that every game might be my last. I also know that in this materialistic world people will soon forget your triumphs. When you perform badly they will only remember that day and all previous successes will count for nothing.

Inzamam-ul-Haq stayed with me in Canada to have a similar operation whilst the team went on to Kenya. The PCB were good to arrange the operations, but overall very unprofessional. After the operation there was no one to take us to our hotel. Our team physiotherapist, Dan Kiesel, stayed for one day, but he could not help two of us in wheelchairs from the hospital. A friend of Inzi's in Toronto called to see how he was, and when he heard our plight he came with his car to take us to the hotel. IMG, the sponsors of the tournament, looked after us and sorted out our hotel and so on, but told us that the PCB had never said anything to them about us. We had been left high and dry. Inzi and I decided that we would tell the Board what we thought of our treatment when we returned to Pakistan. When we limped through the airport, Inzi 6'4" and me 5'5", we looked like Arnie Schwarzenegger and Danny DeVito in the film *Twins*. People thought we were so funny.

What was not so funny was the message I received shortly after landing. A friend of mine said, with great irony, 'Congratulations! The guy who replaced you as a leg-spinner has just scored the fastest 100 in the world!' Shahid Afridi, in Kenya, was on his first Pakistan tour. When the management saw him batting in the nets like a madman – hitting the ball all over the place – they decided to try him as a one-day number 3 against Sri Lanka. He only needed 37 balls to get to his century! From that moment I knew that my time as an international one-day player was coming to an end. It was clear that a leg-spinner who could hit runs as well as this would always be selected ahead of me. I was deeply disappointed because I had been the main one-day and Test match leg-spinner for Pakistan. Having taken five wickets and been awarded Man of the Match against India in my last game before the operation, I knew that I was still able to perform and was not ready to retire. On the other hand, I had to accept that other players were coming into contention. My view has always been that the past is history and people want to see what is happening now. So I accepted the facts and did not show my disappointment to anyone, but I felt very negative for a while. As far as Shahid was concerned, I could only congratulate him. After all, he was playing superbly, and I believe that big decisions in life are not made by us humans, so I could not feel resentful towards him in any way.

Inzi and I went to see the PCB Chief Executive, Majid Khan, and gave him a message from the team physio, Dan Kiesel. He wanted us both to be in the Pakistan squad for the home series against Zimbabwe in October/November 1996 so that he could continue to treat our knees, which were in bad shape. We thought that this would be a good idea too, as we would get the treatment we needed whilst staying in touch with the team and helping in the background. However, the PCB said that if we wanted to do this we would have to pay for our own accommodation in the team hotel. We were very disappointed by this attitude, so we stayed at home and did our own training. I spent a lot of time in the swimming pool and decided to answer them by playing well enough to show that they still needed me. Majid Khan had made a rule that any player returning from injury had to play a couple of domestic games to prove his fitness before being considered for selection. In my first game back after injury I took eleven wickets and was next selected to play in the home series against New Zealand in November/December 1996 under Saeed Anwar. However, I think I returned to the game too quickly, once more, and my knee has caused me problems ever since.

When Wasim was reappointed for the West Indies tour of Pakistan in November 1997 I was still struggling with my knee, but I took ten wickets (five in each innings) in Peshawar. When you are taking wickets people hardly talk about your injury. The headlines all said that I had bamboozled the West Indies and that I was playing brilliantly, but inside I knew that the day I did not take any wickets I would be criticised for my lack of fitness. However, I thought I should keep on playing while I could and, with the blessings of Allah, I would be all right. We won easily in Rawalpindi and Karachi but I only took one wicket in each of those Tests. The questions I faced were polite at the time, but people began to ask 'How is your knee . . .?'

I was selected for the tour to India at the beginning of 1999. Security was to be a major issue, with the political rivalry between India and Pakistan dominating the build-up. Our families were not sure that we should go on tour. Eventually the Indian government guaranteed our safety. When we landed in Delhi six luxury coaches met us, each with curtains drawn. We were to travel in one coach and the others were decoys to reduce the risk of an attack on us! Although we had security people with us, our tour management advised us to stay in our hotels and take security men with us, even when we were dining in the hotel restaurant.

I was struggling with a neck injury that began early in the tour. It turned out to be a pinched nerve in the region of the C3/C4 vertebrae, but I was not aware of the nature of the injury when I first felt the pain. We had played a three-day game before the First Test. After I bowled a few overs I told our coach, Javed Miandad, that my neck was causing me problems. He would not listen to me and said, 'If you want to be available for the First Test you must continue to bowl. Everyone plays through niggles and you'll have to do the same.' I did want to play in the series because it promised to be a very important one for both Saqlain and me. Pakistan were always going to play two spinners because the Indians were unlikely to prepare fast wickets to help Wasim and Waqar. We knew the wickets would be very rough which would take spin. However, as I continued to bowl the pain became more and more intense. I saw the physio during a break in the game and told him that I was getting a pain in my neck and shoulder whenever I bowled. His response was to tell me not to bowl, but Javed would not listen to his recommendation. I was very angry inside, but said nothing and bowled all day. As I was so fired up by Javed's comments I actually tried even harder, and became dehydrated as a result of the high temperatures in the stadium. Needless to say, I was in great pain throughout the night and could not sleep. Then I realised that to play on through anger is not a good thing. Javed himself had played through illness and injury in the World Cup and we had all been very impressed with his strength, but it is not right for a coach to draw on such examples to insist that others should play when injured. Javed often referred to his own playing days and told us that we should do 'such and such' because he had done it. I am not Javed Miandad and would not be able to play on with internal bleeding or some other injury. Sometimes good coaching is not about technique and knowledge of the game; it is about knowing your players and responding to them as human beings.

I had pushed myself too hard and as a result was injured for the First Test at Chennai. The wicket was really turning; Saqlain Mushtaq was bowling at his peak and he took ten wickets in the match. I was not able to play, but I prayed for two minutes after each wicket fell, thanking Allah and asking that we could get another wicket. We were highly excited with the win, especially as an Indian politician in Mumbai had said that the people of India were prepared to do anything to gain victory.

In the backlash to India's defeat, the wicket in Delhi, where the next Test was due to be played, was vandalised. We were very tense, reasoning that if security was so poor that the wicket could not be protected, there was a likelihood of us being attacked.

The pressure on us was extreme, so when the Chennai Test was won we all felt both excited and relieved. I was selected for the Delhi Test and, again, the wicket was really turning. I took two wickets in each innings (Azharuddin, Ganguly, Ramesh and Tendulkar), but I did not bowl well. Saqlain took ten wickets again, but Anil Kumble took all ten wickets in our second innings as they beat us to draw the two-Test series. As a fellow spinner, I could really appreciate what an enormous achievement this was, and it earned Anil my respect and that of many of my colleagues. We never realised the significance of the record he was setting until we returned to Pakistan. India was a fierce political rival to Pakistan and some airport porters asked,

'How could you allow an Indian to create this record against Pakistan? Someone should have run himself out so Kumble could not take all ten wickets.' We never even discussed how many wickets one man was taking during the match – we were so worried about losing that cheating never occurred to us.

The team doctors decided that I should not continue to play, so I missed out on the Asian Test Championship which Pakistan won in March 1999. When I came home I had to wear a neck collar even when I slept. The pain was so intense I would often weep – it felt like a trapped nerve, with sharp electricity stabbing me. My family was very worried, and so was I when I was told by the physios and doctors that the injury would take a long time to heal. As I waited, the pain was getting worse and worse. One day I was sitting at home and Abdul Rauf, a Pakistan team masseur, came to see me. His father had taught him herbal medicine and now he offered to heal my neck. I said, 'Thanks very much, but I don't believe in these herbal things . . . you aren't qualified and you might make the injury worse.' His family had an aromatherapy business and he insisted on sending his brother. I did not want to go along with this, but after a further week of pain I was getting desperate. I prayed to Allah and asked him to take the pain away.

Shortly afterwards, the brother came to my house with some spicy concoctions. He soaked a piece of cotton in a hot 'gravy' he asked my wife to make with butter, turmeric and other spices. The cotton was then placed on my shoulder and he told me not to take it off until the morning. The whole time he was with me he kept telling me that Allah would cure me, not the medicine. Now, I believe that everything comes from Allah, but I did not really believe his treatment had a chance of working.

I slept with the pad in place, woke up and took a shower. The pain had gone completely! It was an amazing experience. I called him and told him that I had no pain and he said that Allah had cured me, but I should still wear a collar every now and then to prevent further injury.

For a month and a half prior to the cure I had done nothing. Sometimes I would sit in my TV lounge and throw a tennis ball to bounce off the wall and back to me so I could catch it. After I took the treatment I was unable to throw the ball two metres to the wall with my right hand. The pain had gone, but I had lost all power in my arm. After three or four days I went to the cricket ground to train, but I still could not throw the ball at all – and then the pain began to return. I prayed five times a day and begged Allah to help me. As the days progressed, the ball began to go a little bit further each time I tried to throw it. Slowly, slowly I began to get my pace back and was able to bowl without being slogged by the youngsters in the nets. After three weeks or so I was almost back to normal. I think this was the worst injury of my career. I did not return to the Pakistan team until the 1999 World Cup.

Salim Malik (1993–95)

Salim Malik was, after Javed Miandad, the most senior player in Pakistan at the time he was appointed captain for the February 1994 tour of New Zealand. I played under his captaincy in the First Test match at Auckland, but had a back problem that was causing me a great deal of pain and had to return home. The problem began on the 1993 West Indies tour when I injured my back in Trinidad. An initial pain began to get worse as I did not allow it to heal. This, in turn, led to problems when I began my career as an overseas player with Somerset.

I did not want to take a break from cricket when I returned for West Indies in 1993, but the pain was so bad that I went to see the team doctor, who advised me that I had a stress fracture on the left side of my spine. The PCB sent me to their doctor in Pakistan, who told me not to play for six months. He insisted that any activity I did was at my own risk and that I should do absolutely nothing for half a year. This was devastating news. I began to think of my father, who always said that if you could manage you should try not to tell your body to stop. He had brought me up with the belief that I should go to work and pay my way in life. I rested for fifteen or twenty days, and then began to worry that I would not be able to feed my family if I was not working. I was the main breadwinner at the time, and all of my money went into my father's account so that he could take care of himself, my mother and my seven brothers and sisters. I was helping to pay for their education too as they studied to gain professional qualifications. Eventually I decided to start training again, and began to go to the park in the evenings where I would not be recognised. I would have preferred to go to the cricket ground, but this was not an option. Unfortunately, I did not understand what a stress fracture was and thought that Allah would take care of me if I worked hard and honestly to care for my family. In April I travelled to England to honour my contract with Somerset and, after a shaky start, I played throughout the 1993 County Championship and was very successful, taking 85 wickets and scoring almost 500 runs.

I was in the squad for the Sri Lanka tour in August 1994 but I did not bowl well. I was not playing with confidence or concentrating properly on my game, and this was not good preparation for the three-Test series against Australia in September/November 1994.

As it worked out, the First Test in Karachi was one of the most memorable of my career. I took four wickets in the game but it was my batting that hit the headlines. Requiring 314 to win, we collapsed to 258 for nine. The dressing-room was silent and full of tension. Pakistan had never lost a Test match in Karachi and we did not want to be the first team to lose there. We had considered ourselves in a good position to win before the collapse and the strain was beginning to show on everyone. I was our last batsman and all eyes were on me as I stood to take my place at the crease. No words had been spoken as I sat watching the game and waiting my turn. Nothing was said now as I left the dressing-room to join my childhood friend Inzamam-ul-Haq. However, I was calm. Whilst watching the game I had prayed to Allah, 'You gave me life. Now please show me respect today as we want to win this game. Give me the strength to play this game.' In that moment it felt that my prayers had been answered. As I strode out I felt no pressure whatsoever. I have been prone to nerves when playing against much smaller teams in matches of far less importance, but on this occasion I was totally relaxed. I cannot say the same for the crowd. People were barely able to swallow as the fear of defeat spread around the ground.

When I reached Inzi he seemed to be quite relaxed too. I asked him, 'Should we slog or play positive?' I was trying to show that he could rely on me, but Shane Warne and Tim May were bowling really well on a turning wicket and the Aussies were 99 per cent certain of victory. Inzi was not really sure which plan to follow, so I faced Warney and took a look at the situation for myself. I took a couple of singles off Shane Warne in my first over and realised that I was seeing the ball really well and moving easily. Inzi was obviously the main player out on the pitch, but I did not think he looked very confident facing Warney. It might not have been right for me to approach him, but nonetheless I went to him and said, 'Look, are you feeling comfortable playing against Warne?' He asked, 'Why?' So I said, 'If you don't mind I can face him. I can play him and you can play the others.' He replied, 'OK, carry on'. In the next over I hit Warne for two fours through the leg side; he tried to bowl me a wrong 'un, which I picked and hit through midwicket. I repeated the same shot for my second boundary and Inzi said, 'You look good against Warney, so you can face him and I'll take the other guys.' We stayed together as the Aussies tried everything to disrupt our concentration. Steve Waugh kept changing the field and Warney, who is excellent at setting fields to his own bowling, moved people around to keep us under pressure. There were quite a few comments aimed in our direction too, although I was too focused to take any notice. As our score crept closer to our target we could sense the rising panic in the Australian team. The final runs were amazing. We needed 3 to win and Inzamam tried to whip Shane Warne through midwicket against the spin. Warne was at the top of his game and he spun the ball square. Inzi lost his balance, stumbled out of his crease and fell over as the ball went past him and the stumps. Ian Healey failed to gather and so missed one of the easiest stumpings ever. I never thought he would miss one like this. It went through his arms and legs and we ran 3 byes to win the Test. Healey sank to the ground and could not get up for about ten minutes. One of the Aussies told me that they had to pick him up and lead him from the pitch to the dressing-room.

I had managed to score 20, and Inzi claimed 58 runs after

coming in at number 8. It was a record last-wicket partnership to beat Australia. It was a big talking point at the time. The Aussies had never won a series in Pakistan; they were on course to take a 1-0 lead and were playing like a team capable of winning the series. The Aussie players congratulated us, but the loss was a huge blow because they had been in such a strong position when I came in to bat.

After the game I spoke to Inzi and said, 'Now that my confidence is high, I can show you how well I can bat.' In the next Test at Rawalpindi I was promoted to number 9 in the batting order and I managed two ducks. The team never let me forget my boast, but thankfully we saved the match to stay one up.

Before the final Test in Lahore one of the selectors came to me to tell me that I had to take five wickets to secure my place in the team for South Africa. Pakistan only bowled for one innings and I took four for 121. Despite this and scoring 14 and 27 runs, they dropped me. I felt I had been hard done by and believed my leg-spin would have been useful in South Africa, who were new to Test cricket and were relatively inexperienced against wrist-spin. It was a massive shock when I heard the news that I had been dropped. I was fielding for United Bank when the message with the final tour squad came through and, for the first time in my life, my legs and body were heavy to me. I felt so sad, but I could not tell anyone. It was the first time I had been dropped by Pakistan and was a very low point of my career; it was a major jolt for me and made me work harder than I had in a long time. I only had one year left with Somerset and I realised I needed to work hard to improve my image – I had been lazy and taken things for granted for a while. I thought I would never be dropped and that I was the only spinner Pakistan would want to use. But you should never think you are special and irreplaceable or God will test you out. I was punished for taking things too easy. There is no doubt about it, I had forgotten my roots and how much my family needed me to work hard; but it was the right time for me to realise the need for a change in my life.

I always try to look for the positive side of setbacks and I vowed to prove the selectors wrong. I spent every day at the cricket ground working hard on my fitness and bowling. I did not spend time with friends or speak to anyone; I just went mad about cricket and bowled in the nets on my own – bowling, running to pick up the ball, coming back to my mark and bowling again – for an hour and a half at a time. If I did have a batsman available, I would tell him to smash any bad balls so that I would have to run and field the ball before bowling again. My wife and my father both told me not to be so hard on myself, especially as this was Ramadan, the fasting month, and I was not able to eat or drink during the daytime. They said I should have a few days off, but I refused. Each day was filled with praying, training, eating with the family and praying before bed.

My first match after this was in domestic cricket and I took a few wickets, but I knew that my form was not good. I could not find my length and rhythm. I had begun to experiment by gripping the ball differently and changing my action. My hand is quite small so I have to really spread my index and middle fingers to control the ball. During this period I tried to bowl with my fingers closer together. The ball was spinning more but I had no control over the flight. If a leg-spinner cannot control his line he will not be effective so to try to counter this problem, and to get as much bounce as possible, I stretched even higher at the point of release. However, I could not get the action to work for me, and as a result of my inconsistent performances I decided to go back to my old grip and the action that I had been using since 1991. This is how I bowl to this day.

At one point after Ramadan I did begin to wonder if I had a future in cricket. You see, all the time that I had been training on my own I had held on to a dream that the PCB would call me up to go to South Africa. I would imagine bowling to Hansie Cronje or Jacques Kallis, not the anonymous guy who was facing me. When he smashed me with an outside edge, I would kid myself that I had just had Cronje caught at slip. If I beat the bat I would be bowling Kallis with my wrong 'un. Once the tour was underway and it was clear that I was not in Pakistan's plans, I began to feel despondent. I spoke to a friend and even considered starting up a business, but I knew in my heart that cricket was my life and I would never lose passion for the game, so I carried on training. Although I did not get an immediate recall to the Pakistan team, Somerset appreciated the difference when the new 'Slimline Mushy' arrived for the 1995 season.

Although I played under Salim Malik only a few times, I have to say that he handled the side very well. He was a quiet person who was always very friendly, but he gave very little away. I never really felt that I knew him. You never knew if he had any negative thoughts towards you and he would never tell you why you had been dropped. He would always dress it up as someone else's decision, although you knew that Salim must have had a big influence on it. As a captain and team-mate he was very mysterious; however, he created a good atmosphere in the dressing-room and results on the field went our way. The performances may have been helped by the fact that Wasim Akram wanted to prove that he should not have been dropped from the captaincy and Waqar Younis was desperate to show that he should have been captain, so they were both taking out their aggression on our opponents.

Salim himself was a great tactician who could read opponents very well, but he was reluctant to enforce his theories and would not, for example, actually tell his bowlers where to bowl. For example, if he saw a weakness in a batsman and thought Wasim should bowl an in-swinging yorker, he would hesitate to say so in case Wasim went for a few runs and then blamed Salim. He seemed frightened to make decisions in case he was harshly judged. I think he was a little insecure. Javed Miandad was very similar in this respect, but where Javed tried to overcome it through aggression, Salim went very quiet. They shared the same nature, but their reaction to situations was different. Javed would speak out, even if he was wrong, but Salim would keep things to himself. As a result, neither received the unconditional approval of the players.

The rumours of match-fixing that dogged Pakistan cricket in the late 1990s arose during Salim Malik's captaincy. He was accused of winning the toss and choosing to bat on a green wicket and so on, but you must remember that this was in Asia, the sub-continent, where people are ready with accusations the moment that your team loses a game. Passions run very high in Pakistan when the national team is playing and the fans always expect the team to win. Part of this is fierce national loyalty, which spills over into personal criticism and blame when someone performs badly. The media play a big part by claiming that something must be 'wrong' in the dressing-room whenever the team loses, even though they produce no evidence. The other thing to note is that illegal gambling is widespread. Many men earning the equivalent of £3 a day will put £1 on the result of a cricket match in the hope of winning a little more, but when the team loses they realise that they have spent much of the family income for the day and they need to blame someone for their loss. It must be hard to come to terms with the fact that you have just lost the money you were going to use to buy your children clothes or pay the electricity bill, so someone else must take the blame.

Salim Malik was naturally very gifted, and as far as I am concerned he was a gentleman who brought some stability to the team. His teams won most of their games, including seven Test wins out of twelve, and he was one of the most stylish batsmen Pakistan has ever produced.

Saeed Anwar (1996–98)

The Pakistan Cricket Board can sometimes be funny. They make decisions quicker than anything. After the 1996 World Cup, Wasim Akram was accused of being involved in match-fixing of unimportant games and he was suspended, along with Salim Malik and Ijaz Ahmed. He was later exonerated and reinstated, but Saeed Anwar was appointed captain for the home series against New Zealand in November and December 1996. I was to play under him in this series and against South Africa the next year. However, he was soon to be replaced by the PCB.

Everyone could see that I was still limping from the operation in Canada when the selectors asked if I was fit to play against New Zealand. But I was still angry at the way I had been treated and was eager to show that I could do a job for my country. I was actually panicking a little bit too because I did not want Shahid Afridi to take my place, so I said that I was fine. Luckily I took ten wickets in Lahore (four for 59, six for 84). Although everyone was saying that I was back, in reality I was not fit to play any cricket. I put my faith in Allah and just tried to do my best to earn some respect. In the Second Test in Rawalpindi I took eight more wickets, although I was not very mobile in the field.

Saeed is a lovely fellow, very funny and someone who is always good to have in the side. Perhaps his one weakness as a captain is that he wanted to make everybody happy. If a player was dropped, Saeed would worry about how to speak to him when they next met. He would use the selectors as the excuse for the player being dropped. But if then asked, 'Why are you the captain if you have no say in team selection?' he would have no answer. He did not have the personality for a captain and everybody felt that they could question him. As a leader, you have to have the authority which signals to people that even if you make a wrong decision they have to know their place. Saeed did not have this.

His last series during this spell of captaincy was against South Africa. We lost 1-0 with two games drawn, but I managed to take some wickets and get a few runs. My highest ever Test innings was in the First Test in Rawalpindi. I scored 59 and enjoyed a good partnership with Azhar Mahmood, who scored a century on debut. The Second Test was at Sheikhupura and it was one of the shortest Test matches ever. It rained for the first day but the covers were useless. When they took the covers off, the wicket was covered in water. So we had to wait two more days for the pitch to dry out before we could play.

A very interesting event occurred during this tour which caught the imagination of the South African television service. They featured it for a long time in their cricket trailers. These ads showed a slow-motion replay of a ball I bowled to Pat Symcox which went clean through the stumps between middle and off without shaking the bails. Symcox went on to make 81 and took a hatful of wickets in our second innings. We needed 158 to win and ended the fourth day with about 20 for 0. Needing to get a little over 130 on the last day, we were all out for 92 and Symcox was Man of the Match.

After this tour, Wasim Akram was appointed captain again for the West Indies' visit to Pakistan.

Rameez Raja (1996-7)

I had one of the best seasons of my life for Somerset in 1995, but was not selected to play under Rameez Raja against Sri Lanka in Pakistan. The press were asking why Mushtaq Ahmed was not being considered for the Pakistan team; I was amazed myself, but never asked, 'Why?' Aaqib Javed, a very good friend of mine and Rameez Raja's vice-captain, came to my house and told me that he and Rameez had a new structure and they were going to establish a new side, but I would have to make people happy if I wanted to be picked again. It was suggested I would need to ask to be considered for selection. I never mentioned my record (95 wickets for Somerset), but I felt secure knowing that I had been offered more years in England and that, if Pakistan were not willing to pay my wages, Allah would open other doors for me. I believe in remaining dignified and waiting for Allah to decide what should happen to me. It is not the will of the people, but the will of Allah, that guides my life. I would never ask for a favour from someone who is playing for Pakistan; they do not know if they will be playing the next match themselves, so how can they help me? I thought back to my father and the Imam at the mosque who used to read the Qur'an with me and explain the life of the Prophet Muhammad (peace and blessings be upon him). Using his example, I knew there was no point losing my dignity by asking about my cricketing future. I looked everyone in the eyes, said nothing and let them hide their eyes from me if they were uncomfortable.

When I first returned to Pakistan, I played for United Bank and took ten wickets against Habib Bank. Meanwhile, Sri Lanka defeated Pakistan. Again, the press was asking why I had not been selected; as a result I was picked to play against Australia, but, in the aftermath of the series defeat, Rameez was replaced by Wasim Akram as captain. I went on to represent my country in New Zealand, England and in the Sahara Cup in Toronto before having my knee operation.

I was then selected for the two-match Test series in Sri Lanka, in which Rameez once again took the captaincy. Rameez Raja was a very well-educated person from a respected family. He was a senior player, but when he became captain I did not know him well. He was very nice to me off the pitch, but an aggressive captain during the matches. I think that every Pakistan captain plays in the shadow of Imran Khan. They all want to be like him and act like him. However, they should rather stay natural to their own characters, otherwise it does not work. Rameez was very hard in the field. He did not consult well with the players and lacked the 'love' with which Imran tempered his aggression. I think he needed to be his own man a little more and to use his own knowledge of the game to steer his captaincy.

Aamir Sohail / Rashid Latif (1997–98, 1998–99)

Rashid Latif was the captain for the 1997/98 tour of South Africa, but Aamir Sohail took over when Rashid had a neck problem. An incident in Johannesburg on this trip created a number of difficulties for the tour party. Saqlain Mushtaq and Muhammad Wasim were walking in the street when four or five men jumped out of a car and tried to mug them. Both men were hit in the face and injured. When they came back to the hotel, very bloody and shaken, the players met with Rashid Latif and we decided that we were not prepared to continue the tour if our security could not be guaranteed. I should emphasise that our decision was unanimous: we were adamant about not carrying on with the tour. Aamir Sohail went to the PCB and told them that the players had made the decision and that the Board should act. Ali Bacher, the Chairman of the South African Cricket Board, met us and some of our players were very aggressive with him. We had again come to an over-hasty decision: on reflection it was unfair to blame the South African Cricket Board or the country for the criminal acts of four people. Looking back, I now see that we were unreasonable – I would be very unhappy if visitors judged the whole of Pakistan following the acts of a few people. In my honest opinion, some of us may not have wanted to continue because we were scared of the South African team and now seized on an excuse not to have to face Allan Donald, Shaun Pollock and Lance Klusener or bowl to their top batsmen. We would have preferred to go home with a moral victory. The PCB came and spoke to us and pointed out that both South Africa and Pakistan would have their reputations damaged if we pulled out, so we eventually decided to carry on with the series.

We drew the first game in Johannesburg and won the second in Durban. The final game was in Port Elizabeth. I had developed a sore neck and a high temperature after Durban, but was fine to play in PE. The first day was rained off and we began to believe that we could not lose and would win the series. I have learned that to make assumptions such as this in sport is very dangerous. You should always be on your toes. We batted well on the second day and, with only three days remaining, we were even more convinced we were home and dry. However, the South Africans bowled us out cheaply in our second innings and we lost the game. I played badly. I was not looking after myself, my neck was bad, my body was not clear of a fever and I was not thinking clearly. To win in South Africa would have been quite an achievement for Pakistan, but we allowed ourselves to be defeated through complacency and the series ended drawn.

If I am very honest, I did not like Aamir Sohail's captaincy and I do not think he was a popular captain. Nobody was sure of him. He could be very angry with people one day and quite quiet the next. At times he would throw the bat in the dressing-room and swear. I only played a few games under him and, although I respect him as a colleague and was never personally offended by him, I cannot say that I rated him very highly as a captain. He always thought he was right and this did not endear him to the other players.

Rashid Latif is such a lovely character. I know him well and would even describe him as naïve. He is a fanatic, totally crazy about cricket and a hugely enthusiastic supporter of Pakistan. He helps lots of youngsters without taking any credit, but it is hard to describe his personality. One day he will be urging everyone to believe that Pakistan can win every game, the next he will be criticising the management for making wrong decisions and threatening to take them to court. He is prepared to stand up against anybody. If he feels he has to say something, he will speak out against the PCB or speak up for the team anytime, anywhere.

As a captain Rashid would be very supportive of a player one minute and critical the next. This resulted in him getting about 80 per cent support from the players. The other 20 per cent of our support was kept in reserve because we were worried about him and how he would react the next day. I think he was a little too emotional, open-hearted and 'honest' with the media as well, especially when feeling the pressure. TV and newspaper reporters will always ask questions about why a player has been dropped and it is important to field these wisely by saying something like, 'He is one of our most important players, but he needs a rest before the next series and so we've agreed to give him a break so he can be mentally and physically ready for the next challenge.' Of course, you tell the player to his face that he is not performing well and you are dropping him – but that is not what you say to the press because they will have a headline shouting, 'Captain says player isn't good enough!'. Sometimes a simple question would prompt a wild response from Rashid and he would be drawn into saying something in an indiscreet way. He was not clever enough to play the media at their own game.

I have been in the spotlight for many years and have had many dealings with the media. I tend to see them as 'friends', but I am also aware that your best friend can be your worst enemy as well. Whenever I am interviewed I try not to make claims or justify myself because I know that the resulting article will only cause problems. I remember once gaining a Man of the Match award, only to be dropped for the next game. When a reporter at a press conference asked why I had been dropped after such a good performance, I could have used the opportunity to question the selectors' decsion and make mischief, but instead I chose to say that I was not playing consistently well. When someone pressed me for a response about my feelings towards the selectors I told them, 'Your job is to perform well in the newspapers. My job is to perform well on the pitch. Their job is to select the team. If you think I should be playing you should say so in your article. It's your job to criticise the selectors, not mine.' The next question was: 'I understand that you have a knee problem,' implying that this was why I was not playing international cricket. I replied, 'If you know that I have a knee problem, why don't you write that despite having a knee problem Mushy is getting lots of wickets in county cricket? You are sports journalists – you should have prepared yourselves well before asking questions. If you look at my statistics you will know that it isn't a "problem" so this is a poor question.' I am quite happy to challenge the media and have only once tried to use them for my own ends. It was in 1996 and some reporters were suggesting that they had heard hints from the PCB that I might be made vice-captain of Pakistan. I thought, 'Well, why not captain?' I was playing really well and thought that maybe my captaincy ambitions would get a boost from being extra helpful to the media, who could write some positive articles about me and my ideas. My new approach only lasted one day before I thought, 'Hang on, this isn't me. I don't believe that people can influence such decisions and I do not want anyone to feel that I owe them something.' From then on I have seen the media as supporters of cricket, but I know they can create controversy from nothing and I am careful not to help them to do that.

Moin Khan (1999–2001)

When I was selected for the 1999/2000 C&W One-Day Series in West Indies under Moin Khan, for the first time in my career I really felt the pressure to prove myself. Moin was the wicketkeeper and he came to me at the start of the first game against Zimbabwe in St John's and said, 'Just enjoy yourself.' Well, I did not enjoy the first over as I was getting cut, swept and driven everywhere. As I returned to my fielding position I told myself, 'Allah is looking after you. If you help yourself and play without fear, everything will be all right. If you do get hit for lots of runs, no one can stop you having your dinner this evening. There is no need to fear rejection, or fear failure. Just believe that you can bowl the batsman out with every ball.' After that I began to find my line and length. I only took one wicket for 30 runs, but I felt that I was heading back to good form.

From there on I played in every game and earned the Man of the Match award in the final by taking four for 22 as we lifted the trophy. I had to do a press conference; they told me I was bowling beautifully and asked how many wickets I thought I would take in the three Test matches that were coming up in Georgetown, Bridgetown and St John's. I want to describe this event because it tells us how Allah lets us know we are not running our own lives. I told them my aim was 20 to 25 wickets. I could have said, 'With the blessing of Allah I hope to get 20 to 25 wickets.' But I didn't. I said, 'MY aim is to get 20 to 25 wickets.'

In the first spell of the first match I took three wickets, but after that I ran out of ideas how to get another one. The pitches were turning and I should have been able to take many more, but I did not get another wicket until I took two in the second innings of the Second Test. In the final Test I managed to take three, but my return for the series was very poor and certainly nothing like the 20 to 25 that I had predicted. I was working hard in practice, but I lost my touch. I believe I failed here because I had been proud and thought that I was bigger than the game. You should never assume anything. To predict 20 to 25 wickets was so arrogant. This whole event showed me that Allah is the creator and he has the power to say, 'Hold on. It does not matter how good a bowler you are. Without my blessing you won't get anything.' When I think back and hear myself predicting such success I think, 'Hang on. Who do you think you are?' Now I will only say, 'I am bowling well and I'm feeling confident. With the blessing of Allah who created me I will find some success.' Every time I saw the press during those days I was embarrassed. You should never have to feel like that if you are giving 100 per cent and doing your best – and I never do even when things do not go well – but I was embarrassed because of the things I said. I was proud, I did not perform well and I was dropped at the end of the series.

The PCB was not sure that they should play me in 2000, but they decided to pick me for the squad to play England in Pakistan. I was in the team for all three one-day internationals and played in the First Test, which we drew. I was not taking a lot of wickets and the reality was that I was not bowling well, but I was giving 100 per cent. At times like this you really need the support of the players around you to give you confidence. I was trying to be aggressive and kept talking to myself positively, but no matter how strong a person you are, sometimes you need to feel that you are in comfortable surroundings.

Unfortunately, I did not get the support I needed. At lunchtime during my first bowling spell Moin Khan said to me, 'That's it.' I said, 'What do you mean?' and he had a little smile on his face that told me without needing any words. I thought, well, this is my last Test match unless a miracle is going to happen. I knew from my experience in the West Indies that nothing was in my hands and that if things were going in a different direction, I had to accept it. I gave everything, but only took one wicket in the second innings (Saqlain Mushtaq had taken all eight wickets as England scored 480 for eight decl. in the first innings). Danish Kaneria was establishing himself as a leg-spinner; he was selected to make his debut in the Second Test in my place and he stayed in the team for the Third Test. This did not embarrass me; I realised they had decided before the First Test that I was only going to have one chance. I may have been more relaxed had I known that beforehand. I went into the match thinking I had to play very seriously to come back, do well and beat England in the three-match series. Had I only had one match to prove myself I would have thought, 'Well, just give it a go; you have nothing to lose because you won't have a second chance.'

After I was dropped, I knew that no one was doing me any favours, but I also knew that my career was in the hands not of another person but Allah. I read the Qur'an every day and Allah would say, 'I'm running the show. I'm running your life. You have to ask me for support.' My faith was getting stronger.

Luckily I was selected for the trip to New Zealand in March 2001. I did not play any one-day matches and I was keen to play in Auckland, but only took one wicket whilst Saqlain and Muhammad Sami took nearly all of the others in a fine victory. I was not bowling brilliantly, but I thought I was doing all right. However, when we went to Christchurch I was dropped.

The commentators then all began to ask why Mushy was not playing, because the other bowlers did not do so well and New Zealand dominated the drawn match. By the Third Test in Hamilton, where Pakistan lost by an innings and 185 runs, I had lost my confidence. We often see this in cricket on the county circuit, and in other sports: players on the fringes of the side get comfortable on the bench and do not really want the pressure of having to play. My attitude had changed. I now thought, 'How am I supposed to perform in just one game? As a leg-spinner I need a run of games to get into a rhythm. I cannot be expected to bowl consistently straightaway.' I became happy not to play. My view was that if they did not trust my ability, I would prefer to sit the match out and enjoy my life. I did not want to face the pressure of having to bowl so well and win the game for Pakistan as I used to do.

I want to make a point to all players. If this ever happens to you during your career, please do not let yourself down. Talk to yourself and try to regain the hunger to play. Wait for your time to come. If they play you once and then drop you, come back hard again. If I must criticise anyone on that tour, it is me. My attitude was not positive. I was not ready to play, so I did not receive any help from Allah. Mentally I was weak.

However, events off the field in the Pakistan tour party did play a part in my negative approach and in the heavy Third Test defeat. Saqlain Mushtaq had been a match-winner in the one-day matches and had taken some wickets in the first and second Tests. Someone made a decision to bring out another off-spinner and to drop Saqlain and send him home. This seemed ridiculous, especially as Saqlain's wife had just left Pakistan to come to New Zealand on a flight organised by the PCB. I was sitting in my room when I heard the news and I thought, 'Hang on. Why are these things happening to a guy who has done great things for Pakistan?' What made it worse was that his wife would have to turn around and head back to Pakistan the day after she arrived.

I spoke to Saeed Anwar, Waqar and Inzamam and we discussed what we should do. We decided that if the board wanted to drop him we could not do much about it, but we could not just stand by as they sent him back to Pakistan. I went to Moin Khan and said, 'Moin, this stinks. If this can happen to Saqlain, it can happen to anybody. If you have made the decision as captain, it isn't right. The guy deserves better justice than this. If you do this you'll have to send us all home, because we won't stand by and let this happen. If you haven't made the decision, you must make a stand.'

Moin was loyal to the players and he agreed that it was wrong. A meeting was called with the chairman of the Pakistan Cricket Board, Lt-General Tauqir Zia. He was a nice man, but he treated cricketers as if they were hardened and tough soldiers rather than sportspeople. Moin said, 'I'm not captaining the team if this decision isn't reversed.' When we said we would rather go back to Pakistan than play, the tour manager was panicking; but the General said that he would not change his mind. The players met at 2 o'clock in the morning and some of us said we would go back to Pakistan. Still the General said, 'Fine, we'll send everybody back, but I'm not changing my decision.' However, the next day Saqlain was told that he could stay, although the extra bowler had by then arrived. Good communication and decision-making were not a feature of the Pakistan cricket scene in those days.

Unfortunately for me, someone (I've heard rumours about who it was, but I cannot confirm it) told the Board that I was the ringleader and that all of the problems were created by me. So I was dropped for the ARY Gold Cup tournament in Sharjah the next month and the PCB viewed me as a troublemaker, although all I did was to speak up for someone who was on the receiving end of some poor justice.

Moin Khan had potential to be a good leader. He stood up for the players and was willing and able to speak to the management and put across his opinions. In New Zealand he stepped down for the Third Test, saying his knee was bad, and they made Inzamam captain. We lost the match very badly and Moin's career seemed to be over. During the journey home a few of the senior players discussed the situation. Inzi was the most likely to become captain after Moin, but he said that if he was offered the captaincy he would refuse it, as he did not think it was right and he was not ready for it. Waqar said that he would not take this chance to become captain; he suggested we all support Moin. We all thought that if Inzi and Waqar refused the captaincy, Moin Khan would keep it, together with some dignity.

The board did ask Inzamam to be captain for Sharjah and he

refused, as he had said he would. The next person they turned to was Waqar. Although he had said one thing on the plane, he agreed the opposite and took the captaincy. We all met at a friend's house; Moin was very cross with him and told him so. The word 'dignity' was used a lot in the conversations that took place, but in the end Moin had paid the price for standing up to the General and the PCB in New Zealand – a decision that I still think was right. He was dropped from the side and sacked from the captaincy.

Waqar Younis (2001)

Waqar and Inzi are my best friends. We grew up together and played cricket together for many years. We are family friends whose wives, brothers and sisters all share good times and difficulties. The three of us are sleeping partners in a Laser Eye Correction business. We introduced it to Pakistan and our friend Nadeem Amin is the Managing Director who runs the company. However, I have to say I think Waqar took the wrong decision when he accepted the captaincy. He lost the respect of some players, and although Inzi had to carry on his career and I had to keep playing cricket, we were not happy with Waqar. Although we did not say it to him, we felt it inside, and I think Waqar realised that he had acted unwisely by taking over the captaincy for materialistic reasons at the expense of human relationships.

I was selected for the tour party to England in 2001 and during this time I watched Waqar closely. I never felt that he was making his own decisions. He did not have the same dignified and proud manner off the pitch that he carried on the pitch. His body language suggested that the Chairman of the PCB or the selectors were pulling the strings. To this day I think that Waqar could have become one of the finest captains of Pakistan, but the way in which he took over the captaincy meant that he lost the leadership touch.

When I came to England, I took eleven wickets in the first tour match against the Combined Universities. I felt that I was telling people, 'Look, I'm still here and I've come here to play in the Test matches.' In the second match against Leicestershire I took four wickets, but Waqar played no spinners in the First Test. We lost the match, with Saqlain and me looking on from the sidelines. The Second Test at Old Trafford saw Saqlain make the team, but again I sat it out. I was keen to perform; my wife and family were with me and I was disappointed that they could not see me play. Then I was told that I had been dropped from the one-day squad. Waqar, my best friend, was the only person I could ask for an explanation. But I did not talk to him about it. I accepted it because, as I have said before, the blessings of Allah have made me, an average cricketer, into the successful person I am and I put my faith in Him, not human beings.

Waqar never spoke to me about it, but the manager, Javed Saeed, came to me and told me I was a great influence in the dressing-room and that he had seen me help the youngsters a lot, as well as having a good effect on the senior players. I used to make jokes when the dressing-room became tense, and I have stepped in to cool down tempers and mend friendships when disagreements arose. It was good of him to speak to me like this, but I never asked why I was dropped. A number of people asked me why I did not look for an explanation, especially as Waqar was my best friend and I had performed so well early in the tour. I said, 'Look, they've made the right decision. I'm not a one-day cricketer anymore.' No one knew it, but I was supporting Waqar behind his back. Some of my family were criticising him, but I knew that if I sided with my family I would lose my friend. Someone told me that Waqar was being put under pressure from the press to explain why his friend Mushy was in the squad but not in the side, so he had decided it would be easier for him if I was not in the squad. Some people have the ability to make a stand in the face of pressure from the media, selectors and so on. I am a little stubborn like that and will stick to my guns if I think I am right – and face the consequences if I have to. As long as I can justify my decision to myself, I do not feel that I have to justify it to anyone else. I think Waqar was trying to satisfy too many conflicting viewpoints and he agreed that I should be dropped. I can see how it happened; it is in his nature, but I do not blame him for it.

Suddenly, I had nowhere to go. My family were with me, but I was not on the tour. I could have gone back to Pakistan, but I decided to stay on and play League cricket before returning home.

Waqar did not pick me again, but he would often come around to my house. Sometimes he would ask me about who should be selected for the team, and I would offer my opinion but never mention myself. I could see that he was hiding his feelings, and he was perhaps feeling sorry for me. One day he was sitting in my dining room with me and I said, 'Look, Waqar, come here as a friend, but please don't come here as the captain of Pakistan. You know that I will never ask you *the* question. Be comfortable here. You shouldn't feel any pressure. You don't make the decisions about me. If Allah doesn't want me to play under your captaincy, I won't. You cannot harm me because it is not in your hands.' I spoke to him for five minutes and told him that whatever happens to me will happen to me through Allah.

I was the highest wicket-taker in Pakistan that year and the press was full of rumours about me and whether I was injured, or why I was not playing, but I never spoke to them or anyone else about my career. I had, and have, no doubts that Allah was running my life and I worked hard to keep playing cricket for the next three years whilst hoping to receive his blessing. Some people thought I should retire, but my career was not over and the story of my 'return', with the blessing of Allah, is described in another chapter.

7

My Country, My Captains III: Unity at Last

'We are one and we will win as one'

Mohammad Yousuf (2003)

I took 103 wickets for Sussex in 2003 and the media were putting a lot of pressure on the PCB to bring back the 'lost man' of Pakistan cricket for the visit of South Africa to Pakistan. The feeling was that the team should play two spinners, Danish Kaneria and me. I do not believe all rumours, but I had heard that in 2001 Lt-General Tauqir Zia, the Chairman of the PCB, said, 'Don't mention the name of Mushtaq Ahmed in front of me. He is history.' Now, a few years later the same man was saying, 'We need him.'

My friends never heard me ask to be selected. I waited and was rewarded, but I did not play good cricket against South Africa in the October 2003 series. I developed a groin injury in England and could not bowl the second innings of the final County Championship game because I could not run. The physio told me I should take a month off, but I had to go to the Pakistan training camp. I told the PCB I was injured; they offered me a few weeks rest (during the one-day series), an MRI scan and treatment because they wanted me to be fit for the Test matches. I really wanted to do well, but again made an assumption: I thought I could pick five wickets despite my injury. My plan was to get the five wickets, then tell the Board that I was injured so I could have a rest and take my new chance, as they would not drop me again.

Mohammad Yousuf took over the captaincy in Lahore for my penultimate Test match because Inzi was injured. Despite the fact that Danish Kaneria was bowling brilliantly the media focused on me. My 103 wickets for Sussex had convinced them that I was going to produce some 'magic' for Pakistan and the pressure was mounting. We won the match, but it was Danish and opener Taufeeq Umar who earned a shared Man of the Match award. I only managed one wicket in the entire match.

Danish has been a much-underrated cricketer for some time, but I think he is now the next best leg-spinner behind Shane Warne. For a player of his age he has performed very well without getting the credit that he deserves. The problem for him is that Pakistan has such a good pace attack the contribution of spinners can be overlooked. I am quite content to see him play when Pakistan choose to pick only one spinner. He does not need me, or anyone else, alongside him to help him along because he has developed into a very accomplished player. The only time I will offer advice is when he comes to me. He is a sensitive cricketer and reflects on his performances a little too deeply sometimes. My advice to him and all other cricketers is the same: put your hand up when you have played badly and move on. Do not spend too long agonising over events because too much of this can make you an old man very quickly. Besides, if you start to make excuses, people listen to you describing all the problems you had with the weather, the wicket and everything else, but they will not respect you.

Yousuf was my captain on this one occasion only and Inzi returned for the Second Test in Faisalabad, but he remains a key member of the Pakistan squad.

Inzamam-ul-Haq (2003-4, 2005)

At the end of the Lahore Test in October 2003, my groin injury was beginning to affect my bowling as well as my ability to sprint in the field, so I decided to withdraw from the Second Test. However, with a number of players injured I was asked to play in Faisalabad. I told Inzi about my groin, but he said I needed to play so I agreed that I would. I was secretly hoping that I could take some wickets and force my way back in to the team for the next series. I only took two wickets and performed poorly. My plan to take five wickets and impress the PCB had failed and Allah had taught me a lesson once more.

I had a very successful 2005 season in England and many people began to suggest that, with my experience against English batsmen, I should be involved in the Pakistan squad for the England tour of Pakistan in November/December 2005. I was not sure what was going to happen and I had agreed to return to England to work for Sky Sports as a studio pundit. When I heard our coach, Bob Woolmer, make a statement in Pakistan that we were going to go with two leg-spinners, I began to think that I might have a chance and told Sky I would stay in Pakistan if selected. When I returned home, my wife was not very happy at the prospect of me leaving home for another couple of months and told me that I should stay with the family even if I was not picked. As always, she was right and I asked my agent to tell Barney Francis at Sky that I would not be available. This was very late notice for them and I regret that, but they were very understanding and my wife was happy that I had put my family ahead of financial considerations.

At the end of September I was invited to a training camp along with about 25 other players. I felt really enthusiastic about the whole situation and threw myself into all aspects of training. Whenever I could I spoke to Bob Woolmer and the other senior players and I helped the batsmen by throwing balls down to them and offering advice. I really enjoyed introducing and leading drills that I had learned at Sussex. The Pakistan players had not used a number of these and they were keen to develop new ideas. At the end of the camp the sixteen-man squad was announced and I had made the cut. Once we got together as a squad I spent a lot of time talking about the English players during our team meetings. We have computer and video facilities in our meeting room and we would review highlights of England's performances in the 2005 Ashes series. In the 90-minute meetings we would note who the quick fielders were, any weaknesses in batting techniques and any bowlers we might exploit. The players seemed to appreciate my input and Bob approached me during the First Test in Multan to ask if I would like to be his

Assistant Coach. I thought about it for a short while and decided that I would. I know my playing career is coming to an end and I think I have some of the man-management skills needed to be a coach. This would be a superb opportunity for me. The chairman of the PCB spoke to me about it and I took on the role with immediate effect.

In addition to helping the bowlers, I acted as an interpreter in the meetings when Bob, or a player with limited English, could not make himself understood. The partnership worked really well and we won both the Test and the one-day series. At the end of the series Bob asked if I would sign up as Assistant Coach for one year up to the World Cup, but I told him that I had another year at Sussex and I did not want to miss out on that because I still enjoy playing. He said that it was entirely up to me, so I suggested that I would like to do the job whenever I was available and he agreed to that arrangement. Inzi and the boys were delighted because they had enjoyed having me around.

My style when coaching is to see myself as a servant rather than a master. I try to win the hearts of the players and I explain very clearly that I may have played for years, but my time as a player is over and I am there to support the younger players, not to 'lord' it over them as a senior. I found myself fetching water, arranging chairs, organising ice packs and creating activities for the players to make sure that they were in the best frame of mind to perform. I can give you an example of the kind of thing I would do to support players in this way. Shoaib Akhtar sat in the dressing-room for a whole day in Lahore as we batted. He did not do anything, but I knew that a fast bowler should have a run around every now and then. I felt that he would be reluctant to just go for a run, so I went over to him and said, 'Shoaib, where are you going to eat this evening?' He said, 'I'm not sure, but I'm going to have a big meal because I'm very hungry.' I told him that I was really hungry too and asked, 'Why don't we go together, but do a few laps first to get a sweat going and then we can really enjoy the meal?' Shoaib initially agreed, but then changed his mind. So I suggested that he put on his spikes and bowl a couple of overs at full pace in the nets to get his rhythm ready for the next day.

He liked that idea and we went to the nets where he bowled three or four overs rather than the two I suggested. I am certain that, had I marched up to him as the Assistant Coach and told him to run some laps or bowl in the nets, he would have done so, but begrudgingly. I was sure that my approach worked when he thanked me after the nets. I had found the right way to persuade him and he had worked enthusiastically.

All coaches must find a way to the players' hearts if they want to get the best performances from them. This is especially the case when someone performs badly. At these times the coach has to spend more time with the player, not less. Mohammad Yousuf only managed 5 and 16 in the First Test and was very downhearted, so I went to him and told him 'No one expects you to perform really well every game.' I knew that he was feeling some pressure because he had been a Christian when he first joined the Pakistan team and he announced his conversion to Islam in September 2005. I was his room-mate when we were younger and, as Yousuf Youhana, he read the Bible every morning because it helped his cricket. His wife was also a Christian so the conversion had caused a lot of heart-searching. The announcement of his conversion was made in the press just before the match, and his parents and the whole Christian community were angry with him. Yousuf is a sensitive guy and he told me he was worried that his poor form would be blamed on his change of religion. I told him he should avoid reading the press and forget about any pressure from this world. His religious choice has nothing to do with his sport, but everything to do with preparing for the next world, and he should separate the two things. After our conversation I took him to the nets for five days of practice, made him tea, and looked after him to ease his mind. I kept him very busy and we went to the swimming pool after play each day. Before the Second Test I said, 'Yousuf, if you make a hundred you will owe me a dinner. If you make a duck I'll provide the dinner and I've already made the reservation because I know the meal will be on me.' I was trying to make the point that he could relax. He did not have to feel the pressure of our expectations. He totalled 98 in the Second Test and then scored 223 in our only innings in Lahore.

Bob and Inzi both knew of the work I was doing with Yousuf and Shoaib and I think they appreciated the way in which I took the pressure from them and allowed them to do their jobs.

The Pakistan team has changed in recent years and I give full credit for this to the captain, Inzamam. We had been wrestling with a big ego problem in Pakistani cricket ever since Imran Khan stepped down. Almost every member of the side believed himself to be the star player, and this attitude destroyed any chance of genuine team unity. If a player was dropped, he would invariably go around for five days criticising the captaincy and bringing the negatives to the attention of anyone who would listen. This has changed under Inzi, whom I believe to be the best captain after Imran. I actually think Inzi is the only person who can do the job at the moment. He has helped the PCB to understand that winning or losing is not the only issue. The way he has achieved this is simply by becoming religious, winning the players' hearts and leading the team through five prayers a day and Qur'an readings at the end of each day. When the team prays they talk about the Qur'an and what the Prophet Muhammad, peace be upon him, wants from us. When the captain reads from the Qur'an and says that the strongest person in the world is the one who forgives people and the weakest is the one who talks behind backs, it is easy to see how a united dressing-room can be created. When the captain also says that the result is not in our hands and all we can do is give our best, it inspires the team and takes all the weight of expectation from their shoulders. I have seen the team getting closer and closer and recall Shoaib Akhtar in prayer saying that he was praying more for his team-mates than himself. Bob Woolmer has seen this in action and said that the team is doing everything that he wanted them to do, but they are doing it for themselves. I had never seen a Pakistan team praying together at 4.00 a.m., but Inzi has got them up to pray during Test matches. The players will then have a cup of tea and go back to sleep for a couple of hours.

When England came to Pakistan in 2005/06 they had just won the Ashes and clearly felt very good about themselves. I could tell by their body language, the way that they walked, that they were confident of winning the series. The problem with this is they were still living in the past, and winning the Ashes meant nothing once the games started in Pakistan. Michael Vaughan is a fine cricketer and a great leader. Everyone in the squad seemed very happy with him and all of his players give him 100 per cent, but I think that England rely too much on Flintoff and Harmison in the bowling department and depend greatly on Pietersen with the bat.

In the First Test, England played superbly, but I think they began to feel that they had the victory in their hands before they had actually won it. On the last day they needed 198 to win and the England players looked confident. But in the Pakistan dressing-room there was not a hint of panic. We were all very relaxed. During the morning meeting Inzi said 'I believe we are going to win this Test match. If we don't, it isn't the end of the world; we will still love and care for each other. Nobody will be picked out for blame. We are "one" and we will win as "one".' The players took to the field feeling confident and we came off as victors by 22 runs. England had been bowled out for just 175. I was impressed with the bowling of Flintoff, Harmison and Hoggard throughout the tour. Bell and Trescothick batted particularly well too, but after the drawn game in Faisalabad we beat them by an innings and 100 runs in Lahore to win the series. In my opinion, the unity of the Pakistan team was the deciding factor.

The PCB have changed their approach to cricket management in the last two years and this has been welcomed by everyone involved with the squad. The captain and coach have been given complete freedom to pick the side from the sixteen chosen by the selectors. This is in stark contrast to the level of interference in team matters common when I was playing. In those days the selectors and the chairman used to get involved in team selection, which is wrong. This change has been brought about by Inzi and Bob Woolmer, who have a clear vision for Pakistan cricket. Inzi has the ear of the Chairman and he negotiates fees on behalf of the team and protects the players' interests. Bob is a very good coach and an excellent organiser. He has a great deal of enthusiasm and has transformed the way that the Pakistan team prepares, but he is also very lucky to have taken on the role with Pakistan at the point where Inzi is the captain and the team has become religious. I have really enjoyed experiencing the atmosphere of forgiveness in the dressing-room. Sometimes Bob would want to hear some criticism of a player who played a bad shot, because he feels that it is a way of showing passion, but no one will do that in the dressing-room now. We understand that a player knows when he has made a mistake and he does not need us to tell him. If we did criticise, we would be making enemies of each other rather than friends. Having said this, Bob plays an important role in instilling training discipline and he is never shy to say what he feels to individual players. The players have a great deal of respect for him and enjoy the new training methods and approaches he has brought to Pakistan cricket. I know there are some who resent his appointment, but they are mostly ex-players who feel that he has taken 'their' job and they are keen to look for any weaknesses. I do not believe this is helpful and, having spent time working with them, I know that Inzi and Bob are an excellent combination who are taking Pakistan cricket forward.

8

Umpires

'I like umpires because they are human beings.'

I was seventeen when Mike Gatting and the umpire Shakoor Rana had their infamous argument during the Second Test in Faisalabad in 1987. The match took place just three days after my breakthrough game against England for the Punjabi Chief Minister's XI, but I only managed to see it on television.

During the third day of the Test Gatting moved David Capel from deep square leg as the bowler, Eddie Hemmings, was running in to bowl and England were looking for victory. Shakoor Rana stopped the game to let the batsman, Salim Malik, know the fielder was moving while the bowler was running in. He actually had every right to do this, but Gatting was so upset he went straight to Shakoor Rana and confronted him face to face. He could not have picked a worse umpire to do this to, as Shakoor Rana was very aggressive, and he is alleged to have sworn at Gatting who then wagged his finger in the umpire's face. In the end, play was abandoned for that day and the whole episode was analysed in great detail by the media.

I felt a bit sorry for Shakoor Rana, but I totally understood where Mike Gatting was coming from. Many people from outside the country realised there was something seriously wrong with our cricket and that conditions for touring teams were unfair in Pakistan. We would prepare tracks to help our spinners because we believed England could not play against good spin. This was understandable and no one thinks of this as anything but 'home advantage', but the umpiring was not great in Pakistan and our officials had given lots of poor decisions against the likes of Gatting, Tim Robinson and Bill Athey.

Umpires were giving England players out lbw when the ball was clearly pitching outside leg-stump. The deliveries in question would have gone on to hit the wickets, but the lbw law states that a batsman cannot be out leg before to a delivery that has pitched outside the leg-stump. I saw home umpires ignoring this aspect of the laws time and again when umpiring England games. To make matters worse, the officials would also 'look after' the top Pakistan players, such as Javed Miandad, both in international and domestic cricket.

The Faisalabad incident was unfortunate because I think Mike Gatting vented his frustration on Shakoor Rana as a result of what had been happening throughout the tour. Our umpires did not communicate with the England captain, and if he queried a decision he would simply be told to get on with the game, rather than receive an explanation. For his part, Shakoor Rana was a strong man who was not prepared to be insulted, and he was the first umpire I saw who was not scared of the reputation of Javed and all the Test stars. If he thought a player was out, he gave it out. I saw him give Javed and Salim Malik out in domestic cricket and, believe me, that would never normally happen because the star players would complain about the umpires, which would harm their chances of progressing.

There is no doubt that normally Javed enjoyed a major advantage when he batted. Shakoor Rana had a poor reputation for many reasons, but in my opinion and in my experience he was a nice man. When I started playing for Pakistan, our bowlers would often be aggressive with umpires and demand, 'Why have you given a no-ball?' but Shakoor would not rise to this. He would just say, 'I've given a no-ball, now go and play your cricket.' He was basically an honest umpire. I think Gatting's argument with Shakoor Rana came about because he'd had a rough time with other umpires throughout the tour and he was very annoyed – with good reason.

I think this inconsistent umpiring also affected Allan Border's Australia team, who lost many wickets to balls that pitched outside the leg stump, though I do not think anything sinister was behind it. In my view, the umpires were 'simple' men, possibly a little naïve, who were influenced by their desire to be well thought of by the stars. This may have suited the Cricket Board, who wanted the team to be successful, but I have no evidence of anything untoward going on behind the scenes.

Umpires in those days were not well paid and there was no career structure for umpiring. They were just earning 'bread and butter' money, so they were delighted to be selected for matches away from home because they could get some expenses and make a little more money. I remember some umpires coming to Multan and staying in the five-star guest accommodation at the Biscuit Factory; frankly, I think the hospitality shown to them was repaid on the pitch. Umpires did not have the benefit of professional training and umpiring classes were very rare. Players and umpires rarely communicated as they do now. I think they were scared to get into a conversation with the players. Unlike today, the technology was not available to put the umpire on the spot to answer for his decisions, so you can see how easily these men could be influenced, even if subconsciously.

This was how things were before Imran Khan started to gain influence in Pakistani cricket. At home we would win every match because the umpires gave us everything, but on tour we could not win a match because the conditions were more even and we were not used to it; the players could not cope. Imran told the umpires to give him out if he was out. He said he wanted to win with honesty, not cheating. He used to say if you get five wickets in Pakistan it can mean nothing, but if you do it in England or Australia then it is a truly great performance. When India toured Pakistan in 1989 Imran demanded neutral umpires. He also asked the groundsmen to prepare green wickets to make the competition as fair as possible.

I cannot mention his name, but one umpire told me, 'Since Imran became captain, our lives are much easier.' When I asked him why, he said, 'Because we don't have to make any decisions other than giving people out who are out. Imran will never question our decisions and we have more freedom now.' Imran played lots of county cricket and he was a broad-minded person. He was not thinking of the present; he was looking to the future. He was ahead of the rest of the nation, and we can now see that this approach benefited Pakistan cricket immensely. We started to go unbeaten in Australia, New Zealand, England and the West Indies, where previously we hardly ever won a Test.

In the 1980s, first-class cricketers did not want to become umpires when they retired, as there was no career path to follow and they felt that they would lose their dignity for little reward. Now the scene has changed completely. Umpires are well paid and sharp-eyed; first-class cricketers are joining umpiring classes to qualify for future employment. In county and international cricket, bowlers and umpires talk to each other all day and after I have bowled a ball I might ask, 'If the batsman had missed that, do you think it would have been out?' The umpire will always answer; usually he says 'No, I think it was going down' (leg side). This really helps you during and after the game. The fact that many are former players means that some umpires can coach you. They might say, 'Your line and length was a bit off today, that's why you were getting hit all round the ground,' or 'It's a slow pitch, you'll need to give it a bit more pace.' The relationship between players and umpires is very friendly, but we still have respect for them and accept their decisions. In turn the umpires know that we will appeal and sometimes disagree with their decisions, but they are not worried by that and stay calm. Umpires are far more professional than they used to be and I have seen a huge improvement in the standard of umpiring during my career. They know that fast bowlers can get very annoyed with them, but they know how to handle them because they have been there. Dickie Bird was always one of my favourites because of the way he handled the players. He was funny and you could question him and know that he would always give you an answer with a laugh.

The players must play their part in cooperating with umpires and maintaining the spirit of cricket. The subject of 'walking' is always controversial and some of the Pakistan team were angry with Alec Stewart when we felt he should have walked in the 1992 World Cup final. The umpire did not give it and we were incensed, because we had all heard the nick and knew that he had been caught behind. We went after him to tell him how we felt, but it was all over in five minutes and I have no hard feelings towards him. International players respect those who do walk before the umpire signals that they are out. Adam Gilchrist is a good example, along with many others, who nick the ball and do not stay in their crease when they know they have been caught. However, umpires get the decisions right 99 per cent of the time so it is not really a big issue, although it looks better when a player 'owns up' when he knows he is out and walks.

I believe that umpires have a massive role to play in cricket development. I have told my Board to use the umpires as talent scouts. The umpires spend every day watching and listening to players. They are in the best position to know who has potential, who is in form and who has the right temperament to cope with pressure.

9

World Cups

'We were lucky – big time, no doubt about it.'

My first taste of World Cup cricket was the Youth tournament in
Australia, when I boarded with the Tipping family. On the pitch,
the tournament was a success for Pakistan. We reached the final but
lost out to Australia, for whom a certain Stuart Law played an
important role along with another young 'Aussie', Alan Mullally.
The tournament was of a particularly high class that year. England
had Michael Atherton, Nasser Hussain, Mark Ramprakash and
Chris Lewis, while Andy Caddick was representing New Zealand
along with Chris Cairns. West Indies had Brian Lara and Jimmy
Adams. Sanath Jayasuriya played for Sri Lanka and leg-spinner
Narendra Hirwani was India's rising star. Inzamam achieved the
highest batting average in the tournament, while I was the leading
wicket-taker. Everything had gone brilliantly on and off the pitch,
and as an added bonus we had started to understand a bit of English.
The only downside from a personal point of view was that the press
did not give me much recognition on this occasion. They saw Inzi,
Aaqib Javed and our wicketkeeper Rifaqat Ali as the future of
Pakistan cricket. I think they said I bowled very well, but there were
no great words and I did not get much of a mention.

1992 Australia and New Zealand
I was not having a great time in 1991 and was not making the
progress I wanted. I was in and out of the Pakistan side because of
my inconsistency and Imran carried me in the squad. I was up
against Abdul Qadir and Tauseef Ahmed for selection at the time.

The start of 1992 was crucial for me: the World Cup was only weeks away and I desperately wanted to make the squad to go to Australia. I was in the squad of eighteen or nineteen players and working hard because the squad had to be cut down to fourteen. I played against Bendigo and took four wickets, but I do not think I bowled very well and I could see that other people shared that opinion.

I suffered a major blow just three days before the naming of the final squad, as the selectors called up leg-spinner Iqbal Sikander. I think Javed and a couple of the other senior players felt I was not performing well enough to go to the World Cup, and in all honesty I do not blame them. When Iqbal turned up for practice I could see he was quick in the field and he bowled really well. Everyone talked about him; he was really impressive and I thought, 'Well, fine, he does look great.' I could see that people believed Iqbal was the man for the job and I thought, 'Well, Mushy, that is it now'. I was sad in my heart because I thought I might never have another chance to play in the World Cup, but I never showed any emotion.

The night before final selection, Wasim Akram told me I was not to be in the squad and I was certain he had read the situation correctly. However, Imran saved my skin at the last minute. He had a very late conversation with the team manager, Intikhab Alam, and I have heard that he told Intikhab that he wanted me in the side because I was a good fielder. I cannot begin to tell you how grateful I am to him, because I eventually made the final fourteen, though by the slimmest of margins. They actually chose Iqbal Sikander as well, so I was very surprised when I was named in the squad and I thought, 'Mushy, this is the time to impress.' I made sure I was the first in the nets and the last one out every day. I really worked hard to justify my place.

The nine teams to play in the tournament were ourselves, India, New Zealand, Australia, South Africa, West Indies, Sri Lanka, England and Zimbabwe. The Aussies and West Indies were the pre-tournament favourites, and the format of the competition was that each team played each other once, with the top four teams qualifying for the semi-finals.

The serious shoulder injury that had prompted Imran's first

retirement was very bad once more and a Pakistani doctor came all the way to Australia from America at his own expense to treat him throughout the tournament. Imran bowled at a maximum speed of about 50mph, but he played every game and still considered himself to be a match-winner. As you will see, he was just that.

We played our first game against the West Indies at Melbourne on February 23 1992, and I was left out of the side for Sikander. It was the strangest of games because we scored 220 off our 50 overs but only lost two wickets. Rameez Raja opened and scored a dreadfully slow unbeaten 102 on a perfect wicket, while Aamir Sohail and Inzamam also struggled to make an impact. Only Javed Miandad's quick-fire half-century gave us a fighting chance of victory. However, the West Indies lived up to their pre-tournament billing and knocked the runs off for the loss of no wickets and with more than four overs to spare. Desmond Haynes scored 93 not out and Brian Lara was on 88 when he retired hurt, leaving Richie Richardson to help finish the job.

This proved to be an important game for me because it became clear that Imran was not happy with Sikander's performance and body language. He had bowled quite well – only going for 26 runs in his eight overs – but Imran felt he should have attacked more instead of looking after his figures as we were on the way to defeat. I received my call-up for the next game, which was against Zimbabwe at Hobart.

On paper, Zimbabwe were the poorest team in the competition and we got off to the expected good start. Aamir Sohail crashed 114 and Javed was on top form again with 89 in 94 balls as we amassed 254 for four. This was quite a daunting total in the competition. Zimbabwe made a good effort in reply but never really threatened our total. They finished on 201 for seven. I felt I had bowled very well, although I did not get a wicket, and finished with none for 34 from my ten overs.

With victory under our belts we felt quite confident as we went to Adelaide to take on England, but we could not believe how badly we performed with the bat during that famous match. We had collapsed to 47 for eight when I came to the crease to join Wasim Haider.

England's bowlers Derek Pringle, Phil DeFreitas, Gladstone Small and Ian Botham were running amok. You would never have thought it at the time, but it proved to be one of my most important innings ever. The weather was bad; it was very overcast and our only hope was to bat for as long as possible and see if the heavens opened to wash out the game. I batted for almost an hour with Haider and then Aaqib Javed before Pringle got me out for 17 with our score on 74. It was a poor score, but our time at the crease saved us. After just eight overs, England's innings was washed out and we gained a vital point from the game. This could only be considered a bonus after our dreadful performance.

With a win, a draw and a loss our future in the competition was in the balance, so it was important we regrouped for our next match. This was a day–nighter against India at Sydney and, as always, national pride was a big feature of the match. However, we also knew that it was vital for us to earn some World Cup points. India won the toss and batted, but they struggled early on. I managed to get the wickets of Mohammad Azharuddin, Vinod Kambli and Sanjay Manjrekar as they faltered at 148 for five. But the great Sachin Tendulkar had come in at number 5 and batted really well. He scored an important half-century during a good partnership with Kapil Dev who, towards the end of my spell, smashed me to all parts of the ground. Despite my three wickets I turned out to be Pakistan's most expensive bowler as I went for 59 runs.

India finished on 216 for seven, which looked quite a comfortable target to chase; but our batting frailties were exposed again as Inzamam and Zahid Fazal fell cheaply at the start of the innings. Aamir Sohail and Javed Miandad got us on back on track, but the scoreboard was turning very slowly and we fell badly behind the required run-rate. Kapil Dev and Manoj Prabhakar bowled exceptionally well and were supported superbly in the field, while we failed to build any more partnerships and lost convincingly. We were all out for just 173 in the 49th over.

Our next port of call was Brisbane to take on the South Africans. Following the loss to India, our future in the competition was looking particularly bleak. We won the toss and asked South Africa to bat. I think we did a good job of restricting them to 211 for seven off 50 overs. I dismissed Mark Rushmere and took one for 35 from eight overs, while Iqbal Sikander, who had been recalled to the side, also bowled a good tight spell. However, this time the weather turned against us. We were on 74 for two when we were forced off by rain. When we returned, the target was reduced by 18 runs to 194, but we had lost fourteen overs. Apart from Inzi, we did not bat very well and our hopes disappeared when Jonty Rhodes dived into the stumps to run him out just short of his half-century. Inzi was recapturing his form, but our World Cup hopes had effectively gone up in smoke.

We realised we had to win the final three games, and even then qualification was not a certainty, so it was with heavy hearts that we travelled to Perth to take on Australia. We were near the bottom of the group and in poor form. We had only beaten Zimbabwe and were extremely lucky to have managed a draw against England. We were now playing one of the tournament favourites and things could not have seemed much worse. We were more or less ready to pack our bags to go home. Even if we were to win all our games, we would still have to rely on other teams beating each other, and the combination of results required seemed unlikely. In my opinion, this was the turning point of the World Cup. We were in a real mess and in need of a pick-me-up. At such times, great leaders show their character and Imran Khan, who still had faith in the side, called a team meeting that was to inspire us to victory. He convinced us that if we beat Australia we would go on to win the World Cup. It was a rousing speech, which transformed the attitudes within the squad.

Before the game in Perth, Imran gave every player a T-shirt with a picture of a cornered tiger. He told us he had worn such a T-shirt in the 1987 World Cup and that if we played like cornered tigers from now on we would win the competition. Many people were shocked to hear the noise from our dressing-room before the match. We were really fired up and were all shouting 'Allah Akbar!' – 'God is great!'

We won the toss and chose to bat first. Aamir Sohail held the innings together with a fabulous 76, which earned him Man of the

Match. We scored 220 for nine in our 50 overs. In reply, Australia lost Tom Moody and David Boon cheaply, but they recovered thanks to good knocks by Geoff Marsh and Dean Jones. Their score had reached 116 for two when I broke through and had Jones out caught by Aaqib Javed. Imran struck shortly afterwards to remove Marsh. I then got Allan Border and the Aussies collapsed, apart from Mark Waugh, whom I eventually dismissed for the ninth wicket. We took the final wicket at 172 and gained the confidence we needed to push ahead. We had fought like cornered tigers and achieved the result that Imran said would come our way. There was a sense that we could do it after all and we prepared in high spirits for our seventh match, against Sri Lanka.

We stayed in Perth for the match and restricted Sri Lanka to 212 for six. I took two for 43 in my ten overs, dismissing Maitipage Samarasekera and Chandika Hathurusingha. A good all-round batting display saw us home with four wickets and five balls to spare. Javed Miandad and Salim Malik both scored half-centuries and it looked as if Imran's prophecy might actually come true.

Our final game was the toughest of the lot. We had to take on New Zealand at Christchurch. Not only did they have home advantage, but were on a roll, having won all their games in the tournament to date. We also needed Australia to beat West Indies later on that day in order for us to qualify. New Zealand looked unbeatable, but Imran fired us up for the game once again. It was during Ramadan and Imran said it was our month and we had the blessing of Allah. He insisted we should not think negatively or even consider losing. He said, 'Leave it to God and we will do all right.' He did not even talk about techniques or tactics at this time; he just created the right mental attitude and gave us faith.

The home side started off terribly and were reduced to 106 for eight at one stage. I bowled my best spell of the tournament, taking two for 18 off ten overs, including the wickets of Mark Greatbatch and Chris Harris. I felt inspired, and I also took a superb low catch to dismiss Dipak Patel off the bowling of Aamir Sohail. New Zealand finally reached a modest 166. Despite stuttering and losing two wickets before we had 10 runs on the board, we won by seven wickets. Rameez Raja hit a brilliant 119 not out to help us on our way, but was overlooked for the Man of the Match award, which went to . . . Mushy! The award meant so much to me because the great New Zealand all-rounder Richard Hadlee was on the adjudicating panel. To be recognised by such a respected player as him was a huge boost for me and I could not contain my excitement after the game. I am never very quiet, but I could not stop smiling or babbling for a while.

I was soon brought down to earth when I realised our World Cup could still be over if the Aussies failed to beat the West Indies. We went into a restaurant in Christchurch and prepared to watch the game, feeling very nervous. The Aussies did the business and we knew it was 'game over' when Brian Lara was run out during the Windies' run chase. When that happened we were all jumping up and down on the chairs and tables. It was a fantastic moment.

We stayed in New Zealand for the semi-final where we took on the hosts at Eden Park, Auckland on March 21. The Kiwis won the toss and batted. It looked like a good decision as they smashed 262 for seven, with their captain Martin Crowe scoring a brilliant 91 in 83 balls. I bowled quite a tight ten overs, taking two for 40, which included the wickets of opener John Wright and Andrew Jones, but there was no doubt we were the underdogs going into the second innings. New Zealand were also helped by the fact that their bowlers did not bowl with much pace on the ball, so you really had to attack, and this was often difficult. It was to prove a monumental day for my great friend Inzamam, but the story could have been totally different if the 'Man of the Match to be' had not been persuaded to play hours before the game.

Inzi was not at all well the night before the match and must have gone to the toilet ten times. He was shy and asked me to tell Imran that he could not play because he had a stomach upset. I could tell that this was an illness and not nerves because his face was yellow and I could see how unwell he was. Although Imran was very helpful to the youngsters, we were in awe of him and whenever he came to ask us how we were we would just smile and say, 'Fine, thanks.' We would not dare to speak at length to him. So I was very nervous when I went to break the news about Inzi. I was also worried for my friend because this was an ideal chance for Imran to drop him. He had not been scoring many runs and the media were putting pressure on the Pakistan selectors to drop him from the team. His confidence was at an all-time low and I remember the team manager, Intikhab Alam, and a lot of the senior players voicing their opinion within the squad that we should play someone else. It did not amount to a campaign against Inzi, but some players thought that we should give someone else a try to see if we could get more runs. When I told Imran that Inzi was ill, he told me to tell him he was playing. He said I had to tell Inzi he was a great player and he could bat down the order if he needed a rest. I do not know why he did that, but I am glad he did.

Inzi only fielded for a small part of the New Zealand innings and went down the order as Imran had suggested. When he came in at number 6 we needed nearly 10 runs an over. All seemed lost, but Inzi crashed 60 off 37 balls and, with some excellent support from Javed Miandad and Moin Khan, we made it to the final with an over to spare. It was a dramatic win because we were all convinced we had lost.

It is also worth mentioning at this point the problems Javed Miandad had throughout the World Cup. He had been passing blood all tournament and also had chest problems. I think it was something to do with food poisoning and he also kept suffering from dehydration. But no matter how much pain he was in, he kept going and he really kept us together in the World Cup. He scored five fifties during the tournament, but he was a brave man to keep playing in each game. He was not fit enough to field for more than about ten overs each match. The rules are quite clear about the use of substitutes, so he would dive after a ball and pretend to have hurt his shoulder or elbow or twisted his ankle. For some reason, no one ever said anything about it. We were flouting the rules, but people were not so wise to such tricks in those days. Javed was so weak that we almost had to carry him to the plane at times, but we needed him badly. He was our main batsman: the player other batsmen could play around while he took control of one end.

In the other semi-final we saw England beat South Africa in a farcical match. South Africa needed 22 runs off 19 balls before they were forced off by rain. When they returned, the poor South Africans still needed 22 runs – but off one ball! It was crazy and completely unfair, but we wanted to play England even though we knew they were a very strong side who had talent in every department. Despite the fact that they had already bowled us out for next to nothing earlier in the competition, we were pleased to be facing them in the final.

On March 25, the day of the final at the Melbourne Cricket Ground, I was so excited that I put gel in my hair for the first time in my life. I just really wanted to impress everyone with everything I did! On the way to the match, Imran played a religious tape, which had great words praising Allah. It was a sort of music with key texts and phrases that said, 'Allah will give you strength, power and victory'. It really pumped us up and we actually put it on again in the dressing-room before we fielded. Inside the ground, the atmosphere really was electric. The official crowd size was 85,000, but I am sure it was nearer 100,000. I just could not believe what I was seeing.

We won the toss and elected to bat, but could hardly have had a worse start with Aamir Sohail and Rameez Raja both falling to Derek Pringle as we stumbled to 24 for two. Imran and Javed met at the crease and there was a massive leg before shout against Javed from Pringle early on. I felt sure he was out – in fact all the team did – but it was not given and he continued to build the partnership with his skipper. The two senior players in our side batted so slowly, it was like the semi-final again. We were on about 90 after 35 overs and had only lost two wickets on a flat track. In the dressing-room we all wondered what was going on. We were desperate for Imran and Javed to play some big shots. The Pakistan supporters in the crowd were actually screaming at them to get out and let someone else come in. You can imagine the scene in the dressing-room; we were all getting very agitated. We need not have worried because they knew what they were doing. They knew we had strength in depth and were building a solid base for us to attack from at the end.

They upped the run-rate and both scored half-centuries before Inzi and Wasim blasted the ball around to enable us to reach 249 for six at the end of the innings. It was a flat wicket, but we were happy and we knew it was a defendable target.

England's innings started as badly as ours. Wasim had Ian Botham caught behind for a duck and we then had a massive appeal for caught behind turned down against Alec Stewart. Aamir Sohail, Rameez Raja and I were almost trying to fight with Stewart and asking him why he did not walk. We wanted to carry on the argument, but Imran stepped in and demanded that we went back to our fielding positions and stay there. Not long after Aaqib Javed took his wicket, Stewart had to go and England were 21 for two. Graham Gooch and Graeme Hick were in together and we knew it was a vital partnership. They were the key men for England and we were worried about them. Imran had said in the meeting that when Hick came to the crease he would bring Mushy on. We had seen him destroy fast bowlers, but we were not sure of his ability against spinners. So Imran called me over to bowl and I was full of confidence because I was not brought on to contain him, I was there to get him out. I felt like a match-winner and bowled at him with a lot of variety to keep him guessing for a couple of overs. The ball that took his wicket was a classic googly. I pitched it just outside off stump and he obviously did not pick it because he tried to play a cut shot. The ball turned sharply into him and he fell to an lbw shout. If you ever see the video of this wicket you will know from my reaction just how thrilled I was. I thought he was the main man and knew that the team were relying on me to get him out. I got Gooch shortly after when he top-edged a sweep to Aaqib Javed, who took a brilliant diving catch. This was amazing because he was by far our poorest fielder and usually struggled to catch a ball hit straight at him.

England were 69 for four and in big trouble before Neil Fairbrother and Allan Lamb helped bring them back into the game. Then Lamb and Chris Lewis fell to Wasim in successive balls and the game swung completely in our favour, with England on 141 for six. Fairbrother was out after a good innings of 62, and I took the wicket of Dermot Reeve, caught by Rameez Raja. Fittingly, it was Imran who took the winning wicket when Richard Illingworth hit the ball to Rameez at mid-off. We all fell to the floor and prayed. We thanked Allah for helping us win the World Cup. I had even more to be grateful for as I became the joint-second leading wicket-taker of the tournament with Chris Harris and Ian Botham. We all finished on sixteen wickets behind the brilliant Wasim Akram, who took eighteen.

Everyone in the Pakistan party was dancing and the young players were shouting, 'We will have new houses.' Most of the squad came from very poor families and they knew that this moment was going to change their lives. We knew if we won the World Cup we would get money and land from the government. Our first thoughts turned to materialistic things and, as you will see, some of us would come to regret our folly.

1996 India, Pakistan and Sri Lanka

We thought we were favourites going into the 1996 tournament. Everyone in the squad was fit and we were very confident. We knew our bowling attack was the best in the world and our batting line-up was as good as any other country's. The tournament was also in the sub-continent and our players were very used to the conditions. In our pool games we beat the United Arab Emirates, the Netherlands, England and New Zealand quite easily. South Africa defeated us in Karachi, but we qualified for the quarter-finals and had to fly to India to play them.

After we arrived in Bangalore we had a practice day. Wasim was not bowling in the nets and after practice the manager, Intikhab Alam, called a meeting. He told us that Wasim was doubtful to play in the quarter-final. This was a huge blow for us as we knew that he was our main weapon with the new ball against Sachin Tendulkar and the other top batsmen in the Indian side. We were surprised and worried when it was said that Wasim had a shoulder problem, because we did not know anything about it. During the team dinner we were told again that we should prepare ourselves to play without Wasim. The pressure began to mount as we realised we would be without our brilliant captain and lead bowler against India on their home territory. We always expected a lot of Wasim and went into the game, under the captaincy of Aamir Sohail, with far less confidence than the earlier matches. Needless to say, we lost badly.

With the right mental attitude I think we could have won the match. India started well, with Tendulkar and Navjot Sidhu putting on 90 runs for the first wicket. I took the third wicket, bowling Sidhu for 90 to make the score 168 for three. During my spell of ten overs I took two for 56, with Vinod Kambli my other victim. We were bowling quite well and the run rate was comfortable for us, but then Ajay Jadeja smashed Waqar for about 30 runs in two overs. He scored 45 from 25 balls and they began to race. During the last six or seven overs we went for about 80 runs.

India reached 287 in their 50 overs and we had a big challenge to face. We were a little bit nervous, but we had a strong batting side so we thought, 'Let's get into them in the first fifteen overs and see where we end up.' In the first thirteen or fourteen overs we were going well and had scored over 100 runs, but then come an incident that everyone remembers. Venkatesh Prasad and Aamir Sohail had been winding each other up. Prasad went up to Sohail and they exchanged heated words. The next ball Sohail hit Prasad through the covers for four, then told him to go and fetch the ball. There was another confrontation, and I think that this was a turning point of the match.

In the dressing-room we could see that the level of aggression was too high. We were in a good position because we only had to get another 180 runs from 35 overs on a flat wicket with nine wickets in hand. We thought we were going to win, but Sohail was still angry and he played a bad shot and was bowled by Prasad. From 113 for two we had a collapse. Ijaz Ahmed and Inzi went cheaply before Salim Malik and Javed Miandad put on a partnership. Unfortunately this did not last long enough. My contribution was to face two balls and get caught and bowled by Anil Kumble for a duck. We were 39 runs short of India in the end.

This defeat was one of the worst moments of my life. The whole of Pakistan was furious that we had lost to India. A special charter flight was laid on to take the team home, and it had to be diverted for security reasons so that we did not go through normal airport procedures. A coach picked us up straight from the plane and we were taken home with just our hand luggage. Some threats had been made against us, and the coach flew along the roads with the windows blacked out to try to avoid problems. I knew the threats were real because a mob had thrown stones at Wasim Akram's house and terrorised his family. Posters of him had been burned in the streets because people could not understand that it was just one of those things; the guy was injured and could not play. One of the sad things for me, as a cricketer, is that Wasim who had done great things for Pakistan had his home attacked just because he was injured for one game.

Rumours abounded that we had lost deliberately. This was ridiculous, but the Pakistan nation was convinced that we would win the World Cup again and some people reacted extremely badly to the defeat. I was the second player to be dropped off and the coach was going to leave me at the side of the main road, a little way from my home in Lahore. I had to call my wife and tell her exactly where we were stopping so that someone could come to fetch me. The coach only intended to pause a few seconds at each location and we were all told to stand close to the door when it was our turn to get off and then get into our cars as quickly as possible. The coach drew up next to my car, which had tinted windows and a number of my family members inside. They pulled me inside and drove me home. Once there I was scared. I thought that if people figured out where I lived and knew I was in the house they would throw stones or firecrackers into my home.

That night I could not sleep. We had two security guards in front of our house, but I needed my wife to reassure me that everything would be all right. For three or four days I did not see the sunshine, as I could not leave the house. Luckily, after the World Cup Waqar and I were invited to play for the Rest of the World team in a tournament in Australia. I was delighted to get out of Pakistan for a while and we both spent two or three weeks in Australia. When we returned home, things had almost returned to normal.

However, rumours that we had thrown matches continued to

circulate. As the rumours became stronger the PCB and the Pakistan government launched an inquiry which I describe later. Despite the allegations, I am convinced that we lost because we lacked confidence after it became clear that Wasim was not playing. It only takes a couple of bad decisions by players (or umpires) and a piece of bad luck for a good team to struggle in any match.

It was very unfortunate that we lost to India because they were our fiercest rivals, but I think that much of the 'animosity' between the teams is hyped by the media. The governments of both countries want to try to show that they are the strongest and the people enjoy the rivalry because we are neighbours and were one country before partition. Beyond the few fanatics who will try to disrupt relationships between the two countries, I have only experienced excitement among the Indian people towards the Pakistan team. During two tours we have been surrounded by enthusiastic crowds eager to catch a glimpse of the players. The hooting and noise inside the stadium whenever we play is exciting for the players and typical of Asian spectators, so we have no problem with that. Recently Indian and Pakistani people have been doing business with each other and there is a great deal of cooperation between the two countries. The border incidents always seem to happen when one government or other wants to divert attention away from something at home. I actually think there is a mutual understanding between the two governments that they need to provoke something every now and then, and war will be threatened, but it need not come to anything. The last time I crossed the border I was treated like a king by the police and border guards. Similarly, when India came to Pakistan in January 2006 a number of the players said that they would like to visit more often because they liked the way they were treated. This is not to say that we do not play hard cricket when we meet. It is always the case that both sets of players want to win our matches more than any others, but that is natural in all matches between neighbours and rivals. However, once the game is over we mix with each other and share a meal on occasions.

1999 Great Britain and Ireland

Although I was selected for the squad, I did not feature in any of the games during this tour. However, I was in the dressing-room for every match and can tell you that I have never seen so many officials and politicians in cricket dressing-rooms in all my life. At every match we would find civil servants and politicians smoking cigars in our dressing-room. The Pakistan ambassador and his entourage would be there and the players often had nowhere to sit down because these people used all the chairs. As cricketers you need a quiet, focused area where there is no pressure and you can prepare each day. The politicians had no idea. They only ever said one thing, 'You guys have to win the World Cup. Our reputation is at stake and the nation is watching you. If you win, great things will come your way, If you do not, it will be very bad for you back home.' Well, you do not want to hear that from politicians and their civil servants, and these things were happening every second day in the dressing-room. Eventually we complained and asked the management to clear the dressing-room for us.

Despite the difficult circumstances we beat West Indies, Scotland, Australia and New Zealand, before losing to Bangladesh in Northampton. After this match, the Pakistan supporters in England went mad. They accused us of match-fixing, saying, 'How come you can beat West Indies and Australia, but cannot win against Bangladesh?' They were not in the dressing-room, but I was, and in my opinion God punished us because we were so proud. We were laughing and joking in the dressing-room after they scored 223 because we thought the match was won. When Shahid Afridi, Ijaz Ahmed and Saeed Anwar were out with the score at only 26, we were still not worried because we thought that one good partnership would win it. We had Wasim batting way down the order and thought that even with four or five wickets gone we would be OK because he can make runs easily.

With six down before we had made 100, panic began to set in. We were thinking, 'Hang on lads, we have to win the game here.' But it was too late because the pressure was already starting to build up. In pressure situations it is very difficult to perform well, even against lesser teams. We had already qualified for the Super-Six phase of the competition, but did want to win this match. God had different plans for us and he punished us for our lack of respect for our opponents.

We qualified from the Super-Six by beating Zimbabwe, despite our losses against South Africa and India. This earned us a semi-final against New Zealand, which we won by nine wickets at Old Trafford. We lost the final at Lord's very badly. We were all out for 132 and Australia knocked off the runs in 20 overs. I still think reaching the final was a great achievement. After Australia were beaten by Sri Lanka in Lahore in the final of the World Cup in 1996, I went to play for the World XI in Australia. The World XI team all agreed that no one thought that Sri Lanka could win the World Cup. It was a real surprise to me that over 40,000 fans in Melbourne cheered the Australians to the rooftops although they had lost the final. They recognised that getting to the final was an achievement and did not criticise them for losing. Sadly, in Pakistan this is not the case. When Waqar and I saw this, we spoke about it and agreed that those fans really knew the game.

One of my 'foes', Alec Stewart, out for 2 (c. Moin Khan) in the 4th Test at Headingley on the 1992 tour.

Early days in England, before bowling too much at Sachin Tendulkar turned my hair grey.

Appealing against Mike Atherton in a one-day international (still played in whites in those days, at least in England!) at Edgbaston in 1996.

Graham Gooch bowled for
135 (Headingley, 1992).

Taken during Sussex's match against Surrey
at the Oval in 2003. This was a rare loss
during our Championship season. I did
better with bat than the ball in this match.

Previous (left): the guile of Wasim Akram. He
conceals the ball with his right hand to prevent
the batsman guessing which way it will swing.
(right) Waqar Younis. You can immediately
appreciate the power and athleticism of the
great fast bowler.

Appealing for leg
before against
Trescothick in
2001 at Lahore.
Verdict: not out!
I have been
criticised for
'over appealing'
in my time, but I
believe that it's
our right as
bowlers to appeal
– the umpire is
there to give the
final decision.

Our wedding day.

Wedding celebrations. Rashid Latif and Saeed Anwar are at the back, and the happy couple is flanked by Wasim Akram and Inzamam-ul-Haq.

A cool Mushy at home in 1998.

Taunton, 1997, with Uzma and our son Bazal (then aged 11 months).

This was taken in 1994. We are at home in Lahore.

Daddy's girl. At home in 2005 with daughter Nawal.

Abdul Qadir – a wonderful leg-spinner and an inspiration to me. He allied a fast bowler's aggression with the arts of a spinner.

C&G Final 2006, Lancashire v. Sussex at Lord's. Sussex's great team spirit was evident as we won this match when all seemed lost. James Kirtley was the hero with five wickets as we scrambled to victory by 15 runs, defending a paltry 172. I took two wickets for 19 runs in my 10 overs.

Overleaf: Imran Khan, Pakistan's greatest captain. He was a mentor to me during my early career in the national side.

10

The Price of Success

'The way we responded to our success still leaves me breathless
with guilt over a decade later.'

When we won the World Cup in 1992 the government gave us
prime land in Islamabad, a gold medal and prize money. We were
well looked after for the success we brought to our country, but some
of us acted very badly and brought dishonour upon ourselves. To
understand the background to this, remember that Imran Khan is a
unique and dignified man. He never asked anyone to do anything
for him. In Pakistan, there was a rank system where the senior
players would be looked after by the younger ones. It was part of our
culture to look after the seniors, but Imran never asked for a favour
or sought to exploit this aspect of our culture. I once went to pick up
his bags for him, but he stopped me and asked, 'Why are you picking
up my bags? I have two arms and legs so it is no problem for me to
do it.' After winning the World Cup, Imran saw a way to use the
success for positive means. Unfortunately, some of us did not share
his moral strength at the time.

On our way home from Australia, the Pakistan government told us
that they had arranged for us to go to Mecca in Saudi Arabia, where
Muslims pay homage to Allah in the House of God. So we changed
our flight from Singapore to get a blessing during the fasting month.
It was a great opportunity for us to make a pilgrimage to the holiest
place. All Muslims who can afford it have a duty to make the trip and
perform the Hajj, our most important spiritual obligation. We were
not able to complete the Hajj rituals, but we had now experienced
'Umrah', a sightseeing trip to Mecca. We all cried and gave thanks to

Allah for helping us win the World Cup. Although this period after the World Cup should have been the best time of our lives, I actually suffered one of the most embarrassing moments in my life due to greed. To take advantage of our success the players agreed to appear at a lot of receptions, dinners and parties, held by rich businessmen who would put great sums of money into the players' pool in return for our attendance at their events.

At the time, there was nowhere for Pakistani people to get treated for cancer; they would have to fly to the United Kingdom or the USA, which few people could afford. Imran Khan had lost his mother to cancer; he called a meeting to say that he wanted to construct a hospital for cancer patients and he realised that our World Cup win was an excellent opportunity to push his case and raise money for this charity. Imran's idea was to give half of our proceeds towards the cancer hospital while the players would keep the other half, but this did not go down too well with some of the senior players. Javed Miandad was particularly against the idea and the senior players had a separate meeting in Singapore, which I attended. It was agreed that the team would arrange our own dinners away from Imran and keep all the money for ourselves. Inside I was not happy, but I went along with the majority. I wish I had said no, but I did not have enough moral courage.

We were at the peak of our popularity and the potential earnings were huge. This was confirmed when the Prime Minister joined us for the flight home. When we landed in Lahore a massive reception had been arranged. As we left the plane, I could not see the road and tarmac around us. I could not even see the trees; I could hardly see anything other than humans for miles around. It was incredible. They took us around on a big bus and people were shouting and screaming, 'You are the Kings! You have won the World Cup! We are with you!' and they were throwing money and jewels at us for the hospital and our players' pool. It took us almost six hours to make the fifteen-minute journey from the airport to our hotel.

I will never forget that day, for we really were heroes to our nation. Everyone wanted to meet us, but we had already decided in Singapore to not attend any dinner where Imran was involved. It was a very bad idea, which haunts me to this day, but when you are greedy, you always make big mistakes because you are not yourself. When a person gets a million pounds he wants another million – by hook or crook you want more. The youngsters agreed to go along with the majority, particularly as they were not as well off as the more established players, but Imran did not know about our decision to sabotage his idea at first. We attended some functions where a fee of perhaps £50,000 was paid for us to be there. This was split between the players and the hospital.

In hindsight, splitting the money would have resulted in a good deal for all, but at the time we were still unhappy. It was not until we got together for a big event organised by many of Lahore's major businessmen that Imran became aware of what was going on. The business people of the city had set up a huge stage in front of the parliament building and the whole squad was expected to parade on the stage with Imran; but the night before we had decided that we would leave the stage one by one to show that we did not want to be part of it. Imran was set to make a speech to the crowd, and people would come to the stage and fill bins with money, jewellery and cheques for the players and for Imran's cancer hospital. As the speech was made, we made excuses, saying we needed to go to the toilet, or whatever, and we left the stage and went home. Imran did not realise what was going on until much later, but we had taken a big step away from him and would have to face the consequences.

We tried to justify our actions by arguing that if the government wanted a cancer hospital it should pay for one. We were the players who had won the World Cup and we deserved to be rewarded by the people. We should not have to share our 'fortune' with a hospital. I soon realised we had forgotten one thing. The money was not going into Imran's pocket. It was part of one of the biggest projects in Pakistan history: there was no research into cancer and no hospital to treat it, and Imran was the only man who could make this happen. He was not creating a shopping centre or a commercial building to make more money. He was doing this for the poor people so that they could have free treatment. His motive was pure and ours was pure greed. In the space of a few minutes we had lost all of our dignity.

There were a lot of dinners arranged and people threw money at Imran's project because he was a big hero, he was honest, he had a great image and was working for a genuine cause. Once it became common knowledge we had not supported the cancer hospital and had set up our own dinners purely for our gain, our invitations dried up. We were shunned and paid the price for our greediness. Basically, the moment we left Imran on that stage, we received nothing for ourselves. Ironically, if we had supported Imran instead of being greedy then we would all have benefited in terms of cash and as human beings. It became a big issue and Imran was so disillusioned he said he would retire. Many people advised him to captain the team to England, where there were many rich Pakistani businessmen who were prepared to support the hospital project with millions of pounds, but I think Imran was not prepared to do this if he did not have the support of the players. He felt the players had no respect for him, but that was not the case at all. It was just a case of greed and it was a very disappointing episode for all concerned.

When Imran did come to England as an individual he received huge donations for the hospital, and I think the project still gets money to this day. Meanwhile, the Pakistan team who had hoped for appearance money at Pakistani restaurants and so on during the 1993 tour failed to get a penny. It was a big lesson for me, because Imran had helped the youngsters throughout his time with the Pakistan cricket team and he would fight the authorities for their rights on and off the pitch, even if they had not been playing well. The same players he had helped so much had let him down badly. I was one of those players, and I do not know about the others but I still feel guilty and always will.

Imran himself was such a great leader that when the newspapers questioned him about the reasons for his retirement he told them he did not want to continue because he felt that the players were not behind him. This suggested it was for cricketing reasons and that the team was established and did not need him. He did not say that we were not behind him because we were greedy fellows who did not want to share our money with the hospital project. This makes me even more embarrassed whenever I think about it, and once again shows the great dignity of Imran Khan. Many sportsmen have big ego problems, but for me the strong person is one who is willing to stand up and say, 'I was wrong.'

Imran never held the incident against me and I remember training in the Qaddaffi Stadium in Lahore in 1994 after I had been dropped from the international side. He was running some laps at the same time and we stood together for our stretches. I asked him, 'Can you help today, because I have been dropped and I do not know why I'm not bowling well.' But he said, 'There's nothing wrong with your bowling. You are bowling well, but they are not giving you any freedom. Leg-spinners need their freedom. You should stick to the basics.' He then suggested that if I was falling away when bowling I should bowl around the wicket in practice, just as fast bowlers would, to keep my body tall and help to generate pace.

He then said something to which I had no reply and made me bow my head with shame. I will never forget it. He mentioned me, along with a few other younger players, and said, 'I treated you like my sons, and what you did was not great. I was hurt.' Nothing more than that was ever said, but I felt really terrible and still suffer for my behaviour. I have learned that you must not abandon your friends in order to pursue your own interests. Sometimes you may gain material things, but you will not find peace or earn respect.

I did make use of the land that the government had given me, located in one of the most expensive areas of Islamabad. Few players lived in Islamabad and none of us knew what would happen if the government changed, so most of us sold our land within a few months of our return. I continued to live in Sahiwal until I married in 1994, when my wife and I set up home in a flat in the military district of Lahore. I then used the money to have a house built in a private estate in Lahore and moved there in 1996. It was here that my fame brought me a lot of unwelcome attention.

My wife and I were very excited to make the move. It was on a gorgeous private estate with lots of greenery – a lovely place to live and to bring up our family. Before the 1999 World Cup an upcoming actress named Laila had moved into the house opposite, which was owned by a police officer. She was not totally established, but she had been in a few movies in Pakistan. Her presence in the neighbourhood was not very welcome because after shooting her movie scenes she would return home at 3 a.m. and there would be horns hooting and lots of shouting and so on. My other neighbours were average middle-class people, so we were very disturbed by this noise every night in the early hours. Some of us would look out from behind our curtains and see all kinds of goings-on that we were not happy about. I had never met her and had only seen her a couple of times in the daytime when I was leaving for practice, but she assumed I was the leader of the angry neighbours.

It came to a head after some people drove through the estate security gate to get to her house. The residents' association met to discuss the complaints received and the story reached the local papers. As I had a higher profile than most, she decided that I must have influence with the media and I had led the complaints. I think she decided there and then that she would make mischief for me.

One day I was sitting in my TV lounge drinking tea with my wife when Laila came to my door. My wife asked her in to join us for tea. After five minutes she asked if she could use our telephone because her phone was not working. We agreed and after the call she said she was not happy with our driver. She claimed that when our driver was not working for us, he would stand outside her house with other men and look in on her. She told us that it made her feel uncomfortable as a woman. I agreed this was very bad, as our neighbours should not be harassed, and I told her that I would have words with my driver to sort it out. Before she left she told me that she felt very bad about the stuff I had said in the papers. She did not think I was a very nice person to have gone to the papers to say that she should move out from our area. I was very surprised and I told her that I had not said anything of the sort, but she would not accept it. After some argument my wife said, 'Look, we didn't say that and my husband has told you that we didn't. If you are coming here as our neighbour to make such accusations, you must have evidence. Do you have evidence?' Laila said she did not have evidence, but she knew that we did it. My wife did not like that and asked her to leave immediately. Laila complained that we were not being nice to her, but my wife told her, 'You don't deserve us to be nice to you. How can you say that about my husband when you have no evidence?' I appreciated my wife's attitude, but as Laila left she turned and said, 'This is not good for you guys!'

The next day I went to practice in Lahore, part of my preparation for the Zimbabwe series. My wife called me on my mobile to say that Laila had come to our gate and was throwing things and shouting. Our other neighbours were very concerned. In our society this kind of activity brings dishonour on to you, and some people were asking, 'What has Mushy been doing to get this actress to behave like this in front of his house? If she is swearing, throwing things and destroying stuff, there must be something going on!' Once I received that call I spoke to Javed Miandad and told him that I had to leave the practice session to go home and sort things out. Javed said, 'No problem, these things happen.' Inzamam and Moin were listening and they offered to go with me, but I told them I would speak to her politely, sort it out and everything would be fine.

When I arrived home I found my wife, who was very shocked. She told me Laila had been saying all manner of things about my family and me and that she was very worried. I went across to Laila's house and met her brother, who was leaving. I said, 'What's going on, friend? Why is she making such a big issue of these things?' He accorded me respect and said, 'Brother, we know you and I know you are a nice man who goes to pray at the mosque. We know that people have a lot of respect for you as a cricketer and as a man.' I thanked him for that and he went on to tell me that they were having some problems with his sister because she was not very stable. He told me that she had experienced similar problems in the last three places she had lived. Somehow or other there had been problems with things being stolen and fights occurring, and each time it had ended up in court.

While I was talking listening to his explanations, Laila returned, and as she saw me accelerated in my direction. When she got out of her car she came over to me and I said, 'Is there a problem? Why have you been over to my house throwing things and so on?' She did not answer me properly, but just started shouting and swearing. I was very embarrassed because passers-by could see what was happening, but as a man I could do little against a woman who was shouting and swearing at the top of her voice. As I was trying to calm her down, my wife and my sister-in-law came out of my house to see what was going on. This made Laila even angrier, and she threw a flowerpot at my house. My sister-in-law, who was stronger than her, slapped her, saying, 'Don't you dare do that to our house!' Laila picked up another pot and threw it into my sister-in-law's face, breaking her nose. At this, my brother-in-law ran out of my house with a gun and fired it. This was a surprise to me, because I don't own a gun and I had no idea that he had brought one into our house. Pakistan does not have a gun culture at all.

By now I was furious and worried about how this would end. I shouted to all of my family to get back into my house. I told my brother-in-law, 'Don't you ever do that again in my house. This is not your house and I will not have you using guns here!' Laila ran into her house and upstairs while I stood in the corridor downstairs. I told everyone that I was going to call the police. At this, she ran out and drove off in her car. I phoned the police and my team and within an hour the TV, the police and the papers were all there. It turned out that her landlord the police officer was not charging her any rent for the house. Later he came to my house and said, 'Please don't mention my name.' I said, 'I haven't said anything. Your colleague found out that you are not charging rent. Sort it out with him.' I did not realise that some police officers do not have good relationships with each other, and his colleague had used his name in the report, asking how the officer could afford such a big house on his salary and why he was not asking for any rent.

For a week Laila was missing. In Pakistan, the system says that when someone is on the run the police can punish the family of the fugitive if they do not turn themselves in. So the police cut the telephone wire to her family's house and cut off the power. I said, 'Please don't do this – they have children and they haven't done anything wrong.' The police officer told me that Laila had a history of this sort of behaviour and this was the only way to bring her in. I persuaded him that it was my case and I did not want the innocent to be punished in this way or, worse still, taken to jail.

Shortly after, I started to receive phone calls at 2 or 3 o'clock in the morning. In the first one a man said, 'Are you a cricketer?' I said, 'Yes,' and he went on, 'Why don't you withdraw the complaint you made to the police? Sometimes you go away to play matches in other countries and leave your family behind, on their own. This wouldn't be good for them!' My first reaction was to feel very shocked and nervous, but then I said, 'Whoever you are, wherever you are calling from, I will see you, but I am not going to take this case back.' After that I received many calls, all saying that though Laila was an aggressive girl she had a soft heart, and I should drop the case.

A court case was brought against her and she turned up for the hearing. Her solicitor managed to get her bail so she came back to her house, opposite me, but then started telling the papers that we had been carrying on an affair in hotel rooms and that I had showered her with gifts from abroad. She told them that I had persuaded her to live opposite to continue the affair. This was clearly nonsense because, if I were having an affair with her, why would I want to bring her into the house opposite my family? It was all madness! The papers loved it and ran stories with lurid head-lines. They always put a photograph of me next to a photograph of her and headlined 'The affair of Mushtaq and Laila'. In less than three weeks I lost six kilos because of the stress and the disrespect I was getting from my family. My wife's family and friends began to suggest that, although I was a nice guy, these things do happen and maybe the stories were true. At first my wife defended me, but eventually, as the pressure mounted, she started asking me questions. I said, 'Look, she wants to get publicity and has no other way out of this. You must trust me, because I haven't had an affair with this woman.'

As in all sports teams my mates joked about it all the time in the dressing-room, but I was really upset and could not eat for a month. I went everywhere for help to try and sort the situation out. My business partner and friend Nadeem Amin told me that the police were not going to be able to resolve this, so he went to one of the film industry studios and asked a director to do something. One of the main men at the studios ordered Laila to move out of the house within a month. The deal was that in return I would drop the case against her. She agreed to do this, but Nadeem insisted that she gave a press conference. At the conference she said that I was her 'brother' and that we had not had an affair, or even a friendship. This, of course, upset the papers that had been running the story for weeks. When she turned to me with her head bowed, eyes closed and her palms together in a sign that she asked forgiveness, all the flashbulbs popped and the papers were full of that picture the next day. Later she lost the support of her solicitors when she parked her car in the wrong space at the high court and flew into a rage when they told her to move it.

Although the events seemed to be over, I still worried about my family and my own safety for some time. I knew that she had many bodyguards and aggressive men around her and never knew if they would act on her behalf. Whenever I left the house I took a friend with me, and I would not let my family go out late in the evening. Such is the price of fame, but the experience drew me closer to God because He had tested me, and by being patient and keeping my dignity I had come through the situation and strengthened in my beliefs.

My family and I were also tested a little while later. We had bought a brand new Toyota Corolla. It was so new that the paper-work had not been completed and the insurance was not valid, but my wife took it to the local shopping area at about 8 p.m. to get a cartoon video for our children. It was a hot evening and the car was full of passengers: my two children, a nephew and a girl who worked for us in the house. My wife had the air-conditioning on and decided to leave the engine running whilst she popped into the shop, in order to keep the car cool. Our nanny stayed in the car with our six-month-old daughter, but while the others were in the shop a masked gunman went to the car and demanded that the girl take my daughter out of the car so he could steal it. She ran out quickly and screamed. The street was busy and some policemen were across the road, but my wife looked to see our car being reversed and then driven away at speed. A huge chase began, but despite emergency calls no one could track down the car.

My wife blamed herself for leaving the car open, but I told her not to worry because, according to our faith, the car was bought with honest money and we would be repaid for our loss in some way. After nearly a week, the rumours began that it was the film actress getting her revenge. The police knew all about the troubles I had experienced and they wanted to put her name in the report. I told them, 'Don't do that! I have just finished dealing with her. If she hears that I am accusing her of this she will be back in the press straight away and the problems will all come back. It's only a car and time is the greatest healer, so let it go.'

This happened just before we came to England for the 1999 World Cup, and the whole squad were invited to a tea party with the Prime Minister. During the party I spoke to him and told him about the car being stolen. He said that he was very sorry and instructed his secretary to get him the crime report within one week. He also said, 'Tell the local people in Lahore to provide Mushtaq with a car until his car turns up.' Imagine that! The Prime Minister was taking a personal interest in my car theft. I went to the police station in Lahore where they had a car available from the pool of unclaimed cars. It was the smallest car you have ever seen and it had to be pushed to start. After six months my car had still not been returned, and I was getting bitter because I felt that my country was not honouring me. I called the Prime Minister's secretary from England and rang the police when I returned home to try and get my car or a better car as a replacement. However, I then took stock and began to see that I was totally wrong to blame the police, or the Prime Minister, or my country for not helping me out. I had become very selfish and materialistic over a car!

Both of these events helped to set me on my way to a new spiritual awareness. I began to realise that I had to look after myself and not rely on other people, but also that if things were going wrong I should not panic. I also began to tell myself that many people had no house and were sleeping on the street. My wife had bought a small car from my World Cup salary and we had a good home for our family. I stopped looking up at the people with three cars and feeling envious. Instead I looked at those without anything, not even a bicycle, and felt gratitude. This is now key to the way I think, and this attitude steers my life.

11

The Infamous West Indies Tour – Grenada 1993

'It was like a movie that someone else had written'

I was at the centre of the Grenada incident in April 1993, which made headlines around the world. It was possibly the worst thing that has ever happened in my cricketing life and it still affects me even now. We had been playing good cricket under Wasim Akram's captaincy. Although there were issues with his style, Pakistan was successful in a one-day series in the West Indies for the first time. We went 2-nil down, but came back to win the next two matches and the decider in Guyana was drawn. I was not playing in the fifth match, but it featured a very interesting conclusion. The West Indies needed 2 to win off the final ball. Hooper played a shot to mid-on, but the crowd ran on to the pitch before the runs were completed. Our fielder picked up the ball and threw down the stumps for a run out, but because the field was overrun with spectators the umpires could not make a decision, so the match was declared a tie.

After the game we travelled to Grenada to prepare for the Test series with a three-day match against West Indies Under-23s. We felt that we had won the one-day series, and in any case, a tied series was an excellent result for the Pakistan team, so we were looking to celebrate when we checked into our hotel. We had one or two days off before the next game and the nearby beach was beautiful. So Wasim, Waqar Younis, Aaqib Javed and I decided to have a little party down by the sea. It was early evening and dark, but it was still possible to swim. We always ate together in the evenings and we thought that the beach would make a pleasant change from the hotel. We asked the waiters to bring some chicken wings and suchlike to the beach for us and we took a sound system to play our traditional music. People were coming and going around us, as the hotel restaurant was a barbecue buffet affair, and the whole situation was very relaxed.

At about 9 o'clock a short local man came up to us to offer us some drugs. I said, 'Excuse me, no. We're not into it.' At that he left. About half an hour later, Aaqib and I were swimming to the sound of our loud music when two English women arrived on the beach and started chatting to us. They had obviously had a few drinks and they talked to us about England and a little bit about cricket. We were sitting together chatting when two local fellows came to speak to one of them. They both stepped aside from us and continued their conversation for about five minutes some way up the beach. Then one came back to join us. By this time it was about 11.30 and the beach had emptied, although all the lights were still on in the hotel. Suddenly two or three policemen approached us. They were in plain clothes, just wearing shorts and T-shirts, but they had guns and ordered us not to move or they would fire.

We could not believe the situation we found ourselves in. For thirty seconds there was a stunned silence, with the police training their guns on us. We were in total shock. You know how it feels when you lose all the power in your arms and legs? It was just like that. We struggled to stand up, but Wasim was panic-stricken. He rocked a few times as we stood with our hands behind us and then slumped to the ground. As he fainted he caught his head on the corner of a beach chair and it started to bleed heavily. The police left him there, but told us that we had drugs. We said, 'No, this isn't true,' and I said that I was going to get our manager to sort it out. They couldn't stop me unless they shot me, so I ran back to the hotel.

The first person I met was Moin Khan. I told him what had happened and he said, 'Don't go back. Go and have a shower, get changed and stay in your room. I'll take the manager down there to sort it out.' I did not think I could leave the guys to face the situation, especially with Wasim injured, so I said, 'No, I was with them so I should stick with them.' Moin told me not to be silly. He said, 'If they have let you go, you should take advantage of that.' But I was sure that you should stand by your friends when they are in a tight spot; I knew that if I did not go back I would never be able to face them again.

Within five minutes all the other players became aware of the situation, but the manager, Khalid Mahmood, and the coach, Mudassar Nazar, told them to stay in the hotel while they went back to the beach with Javed Miandad and me. When we reached the others, the police had already collected a number of marijuana cigarettes in an ice bucket and they had apparently taken some from the ladies. They were still scratching in the sand, but told us that they had 'evidence' of illegal drug taking and they instructed us to come to the police station with them. By this time it was nearly 1 o'clock; we were still on the beach and Wasim was still bleeding because they had not allowed him to have any treatment. We asked them to let him go and get treatment, but amazingly the police said, 'No, you must come with us.'

We put a cloth on Wasim's head and walked with the women and the policemen towards the police station. We were not very happy, as we were only wearing our shorts, and the women were complaining the whole way, crying and insisting that the drugs did not belong to them. We knew we had not done anything silly and that there had been nothing there when we were on the beach, so we just went along quietly. On the way to the police station we came across the local man who had tried to sell us drugs earlier. The police obviously knew him, so they arrested him and he joined us on our 20-minute walk across town. The road was very narrow at one point and a car came towards us. As it drew closer, the local man pulled away from the policeman holding him and ran in front of the car. I thought he was trying to commit suicide! Fortunately, one of the policemen grabbed him and dragged him aside as the car flew past. All of the police then started beating the poor fellow up in front of us. We were scared now, because we had seen how violent the police could be.

When we arrived at the police station, Mudassar asked to speak to the local commissioner or the most senior police officer. They agreed and gave him a number to phone, but he could not get through. He tried and tried for about 20 minutes to make the call. Javed went into an adjoining room and saw a policeman putting the phone down just as we were trying to get the call made to the commissioner. It was clear to him that the police were deliberately preventing us getting a call out from the police station. Having seen them beat up the local man, we were very concerned. Javed became very angry and at last Mudassar managed to contact someone, but the person he spoke to said that the commissioner was out of the city and unavailable. The policemen had told us that he was at home and the number was for his residence so we could not understand how he had just left town. It all seemed to be very suspicious.

We asked to be allowed to go back to the hotel, but were told that the arresting officers had to look after us and could not allow us to leave the police station. We argued ourselves round and round in a circle, telling them that we were international cricketers representing our country and that we would happily take a drugs test there and then. They took us off to rooms individually for questioning and warned us that if we got angry the consequences would be very serious, and so on. They tried to get each of us to confess by saying that we would just get a small fine. When I told my interrogator that I could not help him, he again threatened me with 'big time' consequences. They taunted us. One said, 'Wasim Akram and Waqar Younis, the captain and vice-captain of Pakistan, caught with drugs. We have the evidence and this is going to make big headlines in the morning, fellows!' We said, 'You can't be talking like this,' and insisted that we were innocent. They continued to refuse our request for them to take samples for a drugs test. The policemen were laughing at the English women, who told them that they were not speaking to us properly and that they were going to get the British High Commissioner to come and tell them how to speak to innocent visitors to their country.

It was a very unpleasant experience. Eventually Khalid Mahmood contacted the President of the local Cricket Association. We were finally able to speak to him at 2.30 in the morning and he came to the police station. He gave the police all the guarantees they needed and put up bail so we could be released.

It was 3 o'clock when we left the police station, but all the world's press met us outside. We thought, 'Hang on, only a few local people know about this incident and it happened just five hours ago. How come the BBC, the British press and the local press are here outside the police station with a bunch of cameramen?' We covered our faces and jumped into a car to be driven away. When we arrived back at the hotel, one of the photographers tried to get in to take a snap of our faces; we heard the commotion as he received a slap from one of our managers for his trouble.

We spent the next two and a half days trying to find somebody responsible to take charge of events. The commissioner never appeared and no senior officers made themselves available. For Wasim, Aaqib, Waqar and me the incident was shameful. We knew that our reputations were being damaged at home and were fearful of making calls to our families because we knew that they would be embarrassed. The photos of us with our faces covered were in the newspapers and the BBC had headlines about the four Pakistani cricketers who had been arrested and taken into custody in the West Indies for smoking drugs on the beach. I could not eat for days, but I called my parents, who asked if the allegations were true. I told them they weren't and they said that they trusted me, so I felt reassured. My wife told me not to worry about it because she felt that everything would be OK; however, we did not feel that we were off the hook because we had seen how the Grenada police operated and we were sure that they would find us guilty. Meanwhile, the three-day game began and we went on to win it comfortably by 111 runs.

As time passed, we began to get more aggressive. After three days we had still not been asked to take a drugs test. We were stuck, because we could not prove our innocence and the 'evidence' was disappearing. Our manager kept asking for the test to be taken, but we were told that everything relied on the commissioner. As he was not around, nothing happened. The team was under threat and we called the Pakistani Prime Minister. He offered us total support, which was far more than the West Indies Cricket Board, who told us that each island had its own laws and they could not bring any influence to bear on the situation. Our Prime Minister told the Grenada government that we were ready to pull out of the tour and that he was hiring a well-known lawyer from the USA to represent us. When the government of Grenada realised that the incident had reached such a serious level, something was finally done. On the evening of the third day, our management called a team meeting and read a document from the police which stated that we had been arrested on suspicion of 'constructive possession of marijuana', but that no evidence had been found and we would not be charged.

Rumours continued to fly around, but we were told not to speak about the incident again during the tour. Our management made it clear to us, and the press, that they would have punished us if we were guilty, but that the local authorities had declared us to be innocent and that the matter was therefore closed. After the series ended we began to feel that the whole thing had been a set-up. It did not seem to be an accident that the policemen arrived on a public beach and decided to arrest us. The two women had told us that the men who came to them just before the police arrived had claimed to be from the hotel and were asking if we wanted any more food or drink. However, after we were arrested the women asked about them at the hotel and were told that the men were not hotel employees. So, who were they? I am sure that someone in the press was behind the whole thing.

When we returned to Pakistan, people at the airport showed their support for us. Many of them told us that they thought that the whole situation was a fake and, thankfully, the headlines were short-lived, although the incident is still written about alongside other 'scandals' in cricket.

12

Match-fixing?

'Mushtaq is the poorest player in cricket!'

When I started playing for Pakistan I had never heard of match-fixing. As far as I knew, there was nothing going on. I did not know and I did not concern myself with these things, to be honest; I just tried to get on with my cricket and would keep quiet if players fell out. Whenever management took disciplinary action against players, I stayed out of it and tried to remain relaxed. However, if players needed me to stand up for them, I would do it.

In 1994 we lost to Australia in a one-day tournament in Sri Lanka. When we returned to Pakistan there were many rumours reported in the press that the match was fixed and I was part of it. I did not think anymore about it, but I was not on the 1994/95 tour to South Africa and Zimbabwe and people were telling me that maybe I had not been picked because I would not fall in with the match-fixers. I said, 'Come on. We're living in the real world here. My form is not good at the moment and if I'm not good enough, I'm not good enough. That's why I've been dropped.' I had no evidence and without evidence I did not believe the rumours. I remember reading in the Pakistan newspapers of allegations that a match had been fixed in South Africa. When the rumours arose again in Zimbabwe, Rashid Latif and Basit Ali said that they wanted to drop out of the tour because they were not happy about the captaincy of Salim Malik and, despite a lack of evidence, they thought matches were being fixed. The media were wild with excitement about the allegations and Rashid was interviewed a great deal. Six months later it was all forgotten for a while, and

Rashid did not refer to it again until the Justice Qayyum inquiry five years later.

Whenever we lost during the next few years, the allegations of match-fixing arose again. In the tea-rooms one man would read a newspaper report to his nine friends and they would believe what was said. Within no time the rumours spread like wildfire.

I did become involved in the allegations in the aftermath of the 1996 World Cup. We had lost the quarter-final in India and the country was in uproar. All the players had felt the pressure of losing to our arch-rivals and some had been threatened and their houses stoned. Inzi and I went to a restaurant with our families for a meal shortly after the World Cup. We had not been there long when a group on a neighbouring table began to talk loudly about us and the 'fact' that we threw games and were involved in match-fixing. Now, Inzi is not shy to speak his mind and he is a big guy, so he was ready to get up and go over to the two men who were making the allegations. I calmed him down and told him that I would go and speak to them. I went over and said, 'Look, brothers, we lost the game. But we are sitting with our families now. How about if you were sitting with your families and we abused you? How would you feel? If you have any respect for us as humans, not for us as cricketers, please don't do these things. Our wives and children are being upset by what you are doing here. We might deserve to be abused for losing the game, but our families are nothing to do with that and should not have to listen to this.' They listened to me for a few minutes and I finished by telling them, 'You are the people who made us kings after we won the World Cup in 1992. If you are so unhappy with our performance against India, Inzi and I will come outside with you and you can slap us. But don't abuse us in front of our families.' My emotional speech won them over and they apologised, which was perhaps a good thing because Inzi was ready to hit *them*.

After we lost the 1999 World Cup, the allegations of match-fixing were made again and I think I know why they received so much attention in the media. I have no evidence for this and it is only my opinion, but it may help explain the events I describe later. The government was under a lot of political pressure. The economy was weak and the opposition and the people were demanding that the Prime Minister should resign. It is often the case that governments in these situations try to find something to take the people's minds off politics. By accusing nine of the nation's heroes of match-fixing, without strong evidence, they made sure the front pages would be full of these allegations for three weeks, shifting any criticism of the government itself.

Saleem Pervez accused a number of individual players of being directly involved in match-fixing. I knew that Saleem had been an excellent first-class cricketer, although I never saw him play. He was from a very poor background, had been in jail for murder, and he and his brothers had criminal records. He accused me directly of match fixing and said that he had been in Sri Lanka in 1994 and was staying in the same hotel as the Pakistan team. We did see him in the hotel and a number of the players spoke to him, because he had been a good cricketer who may have played more for Pakistan if he had not gone to jail for a couple of years. I remember asking him why he was there and he told me that it was a business trip, something to do with cricket bats, which was of no interest to us. So, five years after the Sri Lanka game he told the newspapers in Pakistan that he had paid Salim Malik and me $100,000 each to play badly and organise the defeat to Australia in Sharjah. When I was asked about it I just said, 'Let him say what he wants, I don't care about him. It's nonsense.' But then he made the allegations in court at the Justice Qayyum inquiry. I was summoned to appear in court, and for three or four days the newspapers were full of articles about supposed match-fixing. I was amazed at Pervez' allegations because I do not think it's possible to carry that much money into Sri Lanka. It's against the law and the airport scanners would have picked up the cash in his luggage.

I felt very bad as my father and my family began to ask if I was guilty. I was also the focus of attention wherever I went and I could tell that people were talking about me and discussing whether I did it or not. When I went to the high court it was the first time I had ever been in front of a judge. The solicitor who cross-examined me asked some general questions and asked 'Do you know why we're here?' I said, 'I know, but I did not do it. I played well in that match.' He said, 'We didn't ask you if you did it. Why did you say that? Point to be noted, judge.' The judge then said, 'How come you said that and knew which match we were talking about?' I said, 'For four days I've been getting up and reading about it in every newspaper. They are all saying that I've been accused of match-fixing against Australia in Sri Lanka in 1994. Is that not true?' The judge then said, 'Oh, yes, the allegation is about that match.' So I said, 'Well, that's why I didn't offer different information. I've been accused of fixing that match, that's what I'm here for and I've given you my answer.' At this, the judge said that I was a good cricketer and a nice man and told them not to ask me any more questions. I was very happy then and thought that this was making sense.

I then said, 'This isn't a play. I want to cross-examine the person who has made the allegations against me.' The next day I went to see my solicitor because I wanted to know why Saleem Pervez had accused me of taking the money. I asked him to call Pervez to the court and ask him the questions in front of me. We tried to get him there twice and each time he did not turn up because he was ill. On the third occasion he did speak in the court to answer the questions from my solicitor. We asked him how he could afford to pay $200,000 to fix a match, but he said that another man had given him the money. When we asked who it was, he said that he could not find the man (a Mr Butt); he was no longer in Pakistan because he had run away. We then asked how I performed in the match. He admitted that I performed brilliantly. I have to say that I did; I took two for 34 off ten overs (Steve and Mark Waugh), caught Bevan off Salim Malik's bowling (!) and hit 2 not out. We put it to him that there was quite an inconsistency if I had been paid $100,000 to play badly and then performed brilliantly.

It was clear to me that many players had been accused of fixing different matches and I had been accused of fixing a match in which I performed well. I could not figure it out. Then the Pakistan government became very angry with the players. They wanted to see all our assets. I said. 'That's OK. I'm happy to show you what I have.' They called us to Islamabad and the agencies were all there to check on our properties, income from cricket and other sources, bank accounts and spending records. My assets were scrutinised and no trace was found that I had received or spent $100,000. The *News*, the biggest paper in Pakistan, reported, 'Mushtaq is the poorest player in cricket!' After this my family believed me and I felt that the public believed me too. I still wanted to speak to the man who was supposed to have paid me $100,000 and I was told that the inquiry needed to spend another two or three months looking for him, but they could not find him. They never brought him to the inquiry.

I was in the West Indies when the inquiry report was published. I could not believe it when I heard that they had decided to fine me £3,000 and recommend that I should never be captain of Pakistan or a selector. Some of the other players who had been accused in the papers of fixing a number of matches received no punishment, but I, along with the others brought to the inquiry, had been punished. To this day I cannot figure out how this had happened. I do not want to go into details about who did and who did not get charged because I have always believed that you should not put the finger on other people. If I do not have evidence, I will not accuse people.

I still respect the fact that Justice Qayyum was a senior judge and I would not judge other people in most circumstances, but I do know that he was accused of bias and corruption in the case against Mrs Bhutto and her husband, Asif Ali Zardari, shortly after the inquiry. However, in this instance the authorities managed to find out details of her alleged illegal financial dealings, but with all their resources they could not find any evidence in my case. Despite this, I have a slur against my name and cannot understand how I could be found guilty over the 1994 Australia match. I would not mind if they waited another six years for the man who is supposed to have paid me $100,000 to turn up – if he proved I was guilty they could fine me as much as they liked, but no evidence has yet been provided. When you consider that the rule of law was not upheld and I was punished without being found guilty according to evidence, I am even more certain that something was happening behind the scenes.

The government had fined me, but I went to the PCB and told them that I was not going to pay the fine. They said, 'Whatever happens we just want to finish this business. The judge has concluded the case and made his judgements. We want to draw a line under everything. So pay it and you can claim the money back later.'

A short while later, the membership of the cricket board changed and I never claimed or received my money back from the 'new' board. I had lost £3,000 for nothing. My solicitor said to me, 'I don't know what has happened here, or why they have done this. Do you want to sue Saleem Pervez for libel?' I spoke to my family and we decided we had had enough of the publicity. In any case, the man who supposedly paid me $100,000 had admitted to the court that he did not have a house, could not afford to buy himself shoes and did not even have a bicycle. I chose to forgive him.

I know that players from other countries have been accused of match-fixing or taking money to talk to people about the weather, team morale and so on. The South African Hansie Cronje did what he did and was punished. Herschelle Gibbs was accused; Mohammad Azharuddin in India and Mark Waugh and Shane Warne have all been included in allegations of taking money for talking to people about matches. The cricket board of each country heard all of these cases. Now, whatever people have done is down to them and nothing to do with me, but in Pakistan Saeed Anwar, who is the cleanest person around and has never been accused in the newspapers, was publicly punished by a government inquiry. I want to state this clearly – it was a government inquiry, not a cricket board inquiry such as happened everywhere else. It does not seem right.

The press always came to Lahore Stadium to get information when Pakistan was on tour. If I was not with the team, they would come and talk to me to try and get an inside line. There have been occasions when they have told me before games that the match was fixed. I would ask, 'Why would you say that?' and they would tell me, 'We know!' I would say to them, 'Look, I don't believe this. I'm a cricketer and I respect my fellow players. Either we all do it or no one does it. I'm clean, and in my eyes so is everybody else.'

I have had my financial situation analysed by secret service agents in Pakistan and they declared me to be the poorest Test cricketer. If you play for your country for fifteen years you would expect to have a nice car and a big house; Test cricketers have these, but why would they want to risk everything for a little bit more?

I have no evidence that anyone else in the Pakistan team has fixed matches. No one has approached me and said, 'Mushy, would you like to help fix a match with me?' I have been accused of visiting the houses of bookmakers, but gambling is illegal in Pakistan. If I know someone from cricket, maybe a former player, and he invites me to his house, it is quite possible that I could have dinner with him and some other friends and not know that he is running a book. I have been found guilty by association for spending time with a former great cricketer and a very funny man who, it would seem, was doing just that.

I was in the squad that lost to Bangladesh in the 1999 World Cup in England and people still say that the match was fixed. I can tell you that it was not. I have explained how we came to lose that game in another chapter, but I would like to remind you that Australia lost to Bangladesh in England in 2005. It happens.

13

The Art and Science of Bowling

'Looking after the ball is an art.'

I have spent many years trying to become the best leg-spin bowler I can be. During the countless hours of practice and match play it has become clear to me that good spin bowling is a combination of physical technique and the mental approach that enables you to out-think the batsman. You have to be clever and flexible in the mind and body to succeed.

I am not very tall, so I have to try to get as much height in my action as possible. This is vital in order to get as much bounce as possible from the ball, but the fact is that a high arm action makes it very hard to spin the ball. When I land, I rotate my whole body over my front leg. This gives me something from my knee, hips, back, shoulder and wrist that goes into spinning the ball. Players learning to spin the ball must realise that every part of the body is used to create the spin and the variations.

Leg-spin bowling is my passion and I would like to share some of my thoughts about it with you, but I ask you to remember that you are often your own best coach. You need to try things out and analyse the results for yourself. You have to be honest with yourself and think about everything you do. In this way, twenty minutes of thoughtful practice can be much more effective than two hours of practice where you are just going through the motions.

When I bowl I always use the same grip for a leg break, a wrong 'un, a top-spinner or a flipper. The difference in what happens to the ball comes entirely from the wrist. The secret is to complete the wrist action very quickly. Beyond that, I can describe what happens at the wrist but I cannot explain how it works. I do know that a quick arm action, linked with a quick wrist, makes it hard to read a leg-spinner, so I would encourage you to work on that in particular. You must also concentrate on bowling accurately. Having control of pace, line and length is absolutely essential to the leg-spinner.

At the release of a leg break my fingers will have worked on the ball to rotate it and the inside of my wrist, at the base of my thumb, is facing the wicketkeeper and first slip area. To bowl a wrong 'un I change the wrist action very slightly and at the point of release my wrist is facing the batsman. That's all!

The top-spinner uses a little wrist but has no work from the fingers. It can be easier to read because it is the same pace as the leg break, but it tends to bounce higher. If the batsman does not read it, he has to react very quickly. For a flipper, I try not to work the ball with the fingers. I push with my wrist and my shoulders and release the ball so that it goes straight on to the batsman. As a result it is a quicker ball than normal and it is the pace that deceives him.

Once you have learned the technique and can bowl each type of ball, you have to begin the mental battle with each batsman that you face. As a leg-spinner your decision-making has to be very quick and you have to be able to read the batsman just as well, or better, than he reads you. If someone is trying to play you through midwicket, you have to bowl flippers. If he is looking to hit you through extra cover and the off side you have to bowl wrong 'uns. When a batsman is keen to sweep or slog-sweep you, the ball to bowl is a leg break. A leg-spinner cannot decide which ball he will bowl a long time in advance. He must read the batsman, see if he is looking to use his feet and bowl the ball that is most suitable each time. It may be that you will stick with one ball for most of an over to get the batsman into a routine, but you will then put in a different ball to deceive him.

You must also respect the batsman who cannot 'pick' you, because he can swing the bat, hit you for six and win the game against you at any time. Because of this, I do not worry too much about which players can pick me and which cannot. I concentrate on my own strengths and let the batsman deal with the balls I deliver. After all, if a batsman picks my wrong 'un he still has deal with it once it has left my hand. Players will sometimes let me know that they are picking me by playing with the spin, for example hitting my wrong 'un through midwicket, but they still have to judge the flight and spin of the ball and if they get it wrong you have them. Part of the variation I use is to change the speed and trajectory of the ball. I might bowl flatter and with more speed against some batsmen, but not against the likes of Brian Lara, Sachin Tendulkar and Inzamam because they prefer to play against a faster ball. They don't like it when the spinners take the pace off the ball because they have to work harder and this makes them more vulnerable. Against these players I will release the ball slightly earlier to give it more height and slow it down. When playing against this calibre of batsmen you have to wait for them to make mistakes rather than trying to get them out.

The key to success is to practise well so that you can develop a good rhythm. This rhythm allows you to select the ball you will bowl at the very last second without showing the batsman what you are doing and without losing your line and length.

When I started playing for Pakistan it was quite normal for the ball to be scratched and tampered with during a match. This does not really help the spinners, but the pace bowlers appreciate a little extra help. The law is quite specific about what you can and cannot do to a ball. It is quite legal to use sweat to shine a ball, but you cannot use Vaseline or other artificial substances. You cannot deliberately scratch a ball, but we know that this sometimes happens and Surrey were deducted 8 points for this in the 2005 County Championship. The batsmen and umpires in the 1980s and 1990s had no idea, because some players were experts at doing it. Seam bowlers would like a ball with a high seam, so this would be 'picked' by fielders to lift it. Throwing the ball on to the wicket or scratching it would ensure that the rough side was really rough by the end of fifteen overs. The back of advertising boards was good for this. To get reverse swing you have to look after the dry side and keep it really dry and work hard to polish the shiny side. A scratched dry side will be lighter than the shiny side and reverse swing will be easier to bowl. The thing about reverse swing that makes it so difficult for batsmen is that the ball dips very late and it is really difficult to pick.

The ability to bowl reverse swing developed in Pakistan because the pitches are so dry. The Pakistani bowlers learned how to bowl reverse swing at club level and became the experts at it in the early 1990s. Reverse swing, just like a wrong 'un, is easy to describe but much harder actually to bowl. It comes first of all from a very fast arm action. If you do not have a fast arm you will not be able to bowl reverse swing. The minimum ball-speed necessary is 80–85mph. Darren Gough and Waqar Younis have the kind of low, 'slingy' action that helps to create reverse swing. Waqar and Wasim Akram spent hours learning to bowl reverse swing because on spinners' wickets pace bowlers cannot bounce the ball to intimidate the batsmen. They have to find a different way to get them out.

I remember in 1992, when we came to England, teams would get to a comfortable score of something like 150 for one, but by the end of the day we had bowled them out for around 250. Once the ball started to reverse, the wickets would tumble. Wasim and Waqar were brilliant at bowling reverse swing. When Pakistan was accused of ball-tampering, the cameras would all focus on Wasim and Waqar's hands to see if they were cheating, but they should have spent more time looking at their technique because this was the key to their success. At the time the ball was often given a little 'negative' treatment, and this offered them some help. Nowadays the laws are clear and the cameras are everywhere, but the best reverse swing bowlers, including Andrew Flintoff, benefit because their team-mates know how to 'look after' the ball. This is different to ball-tampering because the laws are explicit and if you are seen to tamper you will be punished. 'Looking after' the ball is an art and it relies on the use of the dry areas of the pitch and the odd fingernail. I do not see it as a problem in cricket. It is part of the game and the umpires have to keep checking to make sure that the players are the right side of the law. If they cross the legal boundary, they have to take their punishment.

All of the top fast bowlers in the world can produce reverse swing in one-day matches and it is really hard for the batsmen to pick it with the white ball. You just cannot see which side is shiny. I really admire the people who increased the range of fast bowling in the game. Fast bowling has become more like spin in the way that the bowlers set up players over a few balls and then capture them with a change. Andrew Flintoff does this beautifully by bowling a few outswingers then producing an inswinging yorker. Absolutely brilliant!

14

Somerset

'You can be the hero if you enjoy your cricket and believe in yourself'

During the 1992 tour, Somerset told me that they intended to sign a spinner and I was delighted. At the time, only Wasim Akram and Waqar Younis played in county cricket. When I was offered the opportunity to play with Somerset, I did not hesitate and grabbed it with both hands.

After the 1993 West Indies tour I was struck down with a stress fracture in my back. The Somerset chief executive, Peter Anderson, met me in London and I underwent an MRI scan before returning to Pakistan. I thought I would be fine by the 1993 county season, but the doctor in Pakistan said I would not be able to play for six months. This was not an option for me because I had the opportunity of a lifetime to play for Somerset, and I knew that I needed to be fit within six weeks. I was so keen to play in England that I tried to swim and jog slowly, but my back was still hurting. I could see trouble ahead, but I was determined not to miss out on my big chance. I went over to England and, although Somerset knew things were not quite right, I said, 'Don't worry, I will be fine.' I had not had a net in weeks back in Pakistan, and the pain was extreme when I was practising in the nets at Somerset, but I just kept going and tried not to show the pain.

Our first game was against Surrey in the Benson and Hedges Cup and I was struggling to bend down in the hotel. I was really worried before the game and did not know how I would get through it. My fears were well founded, as I could not run or move around the field after I had bowled five or six overs. It was very embarrassing when the captain came over and told me that I would have to leave the field if that was the best I could do. The moment I returned to the changing rooms I could see that the coaches were very angry with me. To be honest, I could not blame them. I had batted quite well, but we lost the game and I was summoned to a meeting with the Somerset hierarchy. I met with the coach Bob Cottam and Peter Anderson. They asked me why I had lied about my injury and said they could have signed someone else if I had let them know. I told them I did not realise that my back was so bad, but I would be fit for the next game. I put it down to early season soreness and the fact that it was very cold. They left me in no doubt that if I was not fit they would be signing a replacement. It was never my intention to take advantage of their generosity, and I did want to play every match for Somerset, so I was feeling quite uncomfortable about my situation. I asked God to give me strength and literally begged for fitness. I had never prayed so much in my life.

The next match was over four days against Lancashire and I took five or six wickets and scored 30-odd in each innings. That was the last time I felt any pain from my back. I cannot explain how it happened, but within a week the pain left my body completely. I do not know how or why, but I played through the rest of the season without any pain at all. I had been a desperate man, but my belief in Allah pulled me through. I felt as though my faith had been repaid. In the end I had a very good debut season for Somerset, finishing as the second leading wicket-taker in the County Championship with 85 wickets, behind Glamorgan's Steve Watkin. I also chipped in with 498 runs as we finished fifth, which was a good performance for Somerset.

I remember clearly that it was 498 runs and not 500 because Bob Cottam had made a bet with me. Once he realised that I was serious about playing and we overcame the trust problem that my injury created, he asked if I wanted to bet a meal that I could not get 80 wickets and 500 runs in the season. I took it on and went into the last innings of the last match, against Durham at Chester-le-Street, with 85 wickets and 498 runs. We talked about the fact that I only needed 2 runs before I went in to the non-striker's end. The batsman drove the first ball straight and I left my crease to make the run, but the bowler put his hand out and deflected the ball on to my stumps. I was run out without facing a ball, 2 runs short of my target. I was very disappointed when I returned to the dressing-room, but Bob is an honourable man and he told me that the extra five wickets were more important than 2 runs so he was happy to provide the meal. Having said that he was honourable, it occurs to me that I still have not had the meal. I remember him buying me a few fruit juices, but the meal has yet to be eaten. I'm sure Bob meant well and I have no intention of claiming the meal now!

I absolutely loved my first year playing in Taunton and proved to be very popular there. The management were happy with how the season went, but they admitted that at first they thought I had just turned up for the money. I was just so happy that my back recovered because I do not know what would have happened otherwise. Eventually Somerset were telling me to take a rest because I said 'yes' every time I was asked to play cricket and they were concerned that I might aggravate my injury.

As my first season progressed I bowled more and more overs and began to settle into the dressing-room culture and the national culture of England. My progress in speaking English was rapid – it had to be, as I had so much to learn. Graham Rose picked me up from the airport when I first arrived and I could only understand the odd word he spoke as he drove me to Somerset. Neil Mallender was a great help to me as he would take me shopping and tell me what to buy and what to avoid. He came on trips to town to buy shaving cream and suchlike because I was so 'helpless'. Graham was my room-mate in the first year and he asked me lots of questions when he saw me praying. I told him that I was asking to be injury-free and to help Somerset to be successful and he understood that this helped my cricket. As the season progressed, I adjusted to the people around me and felt like a local rather than the overseas player.

Once in the nets, I began to see that the culture of cricket was also different to Pakistan. Thankfully, I have always been blessed with the ability to observe and learn, so I could see a difference in the way that net practice was conducted. In Pakistan, when a batsman plays the ball into the netting the bowler will go and get it. I did this for the first couple of sessions, then realised that the batsmen show respect for the bowlers by picking up the ball and tossing it back to the bowler. This makes a big difference to the bowlers as it saves so much energy. The difference in culture also applied to the level of professionalism and expectation in England. Back home in Pakistan, first-class cricketers had jobs for life with the banks and big companies. This meant that the players did not feel the urgent need to play well in order to secure a new contract. At Somerset, a player who performed badly would be in the nets early the next day with a coach to try to iron out any weaknesses. In Pakistan a player in a similar position would probably take the morning off. Training and match play in Somerset were organised and assessed far more professionally than performances for United Bank, but I understood the situation and settled in to it quite comfortably after a month or so.

During my time with Somerset I closely followed the progress of our young opening batsman, Marcus Trescothick, along with a very talented batsman named Mark Lathwell. Lathwell had much more natural ability than Trescothick and could have gone on to become one of England's leading batsmen for years, but he never believed in himself. I would chat to him and tell him to give everything whilst staying relaxed. I told him not to worry about the result, but he just did not have the temperament to make it. It is a great shame that he has drifted out of the first-class game. Trescothick was the complete opposite; he was not as talented as Lathwell, but he had passion and was always playing around with a bat and ball. At first he carried a lot of weight and would regularly get dropped from the first team, but he was a very happy person and would not let anything get him down too easily. He was always asking questions about every aspect of the game, and he would grab the wicketkeeping gloves and ask me to bowl my different leg-spin variations to him so he could learn how to read and play them. I was so impressed with this guy's attitude, passion and hunger. He would even come round to my house and want to play about with a tennis ball.

Trescothick would also do anything for his team-mates. Nothing was too much trouble. He took my advice to respect the older players as a long-term investment because he would get respect back and this can be seen every day now. He has the most remarkable body language. You can tell he is not scared of failure and he is not weighed down by expectations put on him. He is not worried by the thought of facing the quickest bowler or the best spinner, and that is a rare quality. It is a joy to watch him do well. I must admit I am a little surprised at how he has taken the international scene by such storm, but I am really pleased for him.

Other players who could have benefited from such an outlook are Graeme Hick and Mark Ramprakash, two fine players who have never done a lot at international level because you can tell they are uncomfortable. I have bowled at them many times and you can see they are not happy or acting naturally when they are playing for their country. In county cricket they are awesome, but they have put too many shackles on themselves to be successful at the top level. If you have a bit of talent, make sure that you have a big heart to go with it. Aim for the top and you can be a better player than a team-mate with more natural ability. You can be the hero if you enjoy your cricket and believe in yourself; Marcus Trescothick is the best example I can give you of that.

Andy Caddick was similar to Trescothick in that he made the most of what talent he had. When I first played with him he had not qualified to play for England, but he could play county cricket. I admired him as a great bowler and he had the right attitude for a fast bowler. He never worried about an opponent because he believed he was better than the batsman at the other end and always felt he could get him out. This outlook has served him well, and we forged a great partnership because we had the same attitude. I felt I should be the match-winner for Somerset, not Andy Caddick, and he felt the same; it meant we spurred each other on to achieve more. As a pair we won many games for Somerset.

Unfortunately Caddick carried his attitude off the pitch, which did not make him the most popular person. It is not a good idea to consider yourself the best once you have walked past the boundary rope. If you have won the game with a century or seven wickets you should put it behind you, as people do not want to hear about it. So, in a sense, Caddick was not very popular in the dressing-room. He would help you out if you needed something, but every now and again he would treat people as though he were superior to them.

Being a successful cricketer and a successful human being relies on getting the balance right. As I spent more time in England and Somerset I began to lose my balance and would come close to falling a long way down.

15

Losing My Way

'When you cross the rope at the end of the game, you are just another ordinary person and you need to learn about life.'

During the 1993 season I was very keen to join in with the dressing-room culture at Somerset. Things were going well on the field, my English was improving steadily and I was the centre of attention at the county club. Although I was engaged to be married, my fiancée was in Pakistan and I had lots of free time in the evenings. As a young man 'alone' in the West for the first time I enjoyed a social life with the other players. I actually began to live like a European. I had been brought up to pray five times a day, but by August and September I was missing one or two prayers a day. It is possible to catch up a missed prayer the next day, but I was not doing this either. I never stopped reading the Qur'an each morning and completing my first prayer, but I became lazy. I did feel guilty at times, but I was having such a good time, my cricket was successful and I thought that everything would be fine.

My second season at Somerset was interrupted after a couple of months because I had to represent Pakistan against Sri Lanka; nevertheless it was quite a successful season. I was able to contribute to dressing-room discussions as my English was much improved and I produced a number of good performances. The best was an eleven-wicket haul in my last match of the season against Worcestershire, my victims including Graeme Hick and Tom Moody. Unfortunately I continued to enjoy my social time and developed a routine of playing cricket, going out with the boys, coming home to sleep and then back to cricket. Prayers were becoming rare, and I was becoming more uncomfortable because I knew that I was not observing the Five Pillars of Islam. I was not sleeping well, but could not break the cycle.

I should mention the Five Pillars of Islam here as they may help you to understand the sacrifices and devotion expected of a Muslim. The first pillar is 'Iman': to have faith in God and to follow the teachings of Muhammad, the final prophet. The second is 'Salah': to pray five times each day. 'Zakah', or charity, is the third pillar and to observe this we must support our family, friends and neighbours who are in need. During Ramadan Muslims must fast between the hours of sunrise and sunset. This means that during daylight hours we can only drink water. It is possible to miss five days for a Test match and make them up later, but this is not really necessary. In South Africa we once played a Test match during Ramadan and on the last day they needed to get eight wickets to win. We had seven guys in the team who were up at 4.30 a.m. to eat and then fasted during the day, but their performances were not affected. In fact I think we play better at these times because we feel supported by our faith. The fifth pillar is 'Hajj'. This is the obligation to make the pilgrimage to Mecca if you are able. I managed to complete this in 2004 alongside Saeed Anwar and many others under the guidance of the teacher and scholar, Maulana Tariq Jamil. It is a highlight of my life and a journey that I hope to repeat many times.

My new wife came to join me in 1994, but returned home after a short while because she was not enjoying the lifestyle in England. She had no friends in Somerset and spoke little English. She was also a shy person, and I did not help the situation because I would go out with my friends after cricket rather than go home to spend time with her. When I did take her out to a bar or restaurant with other team members, she found it difficult to accept the way in which men and women socialised together. The 'freedom' that people accept as normal in England is frowned upon in our culture and she was shocked to see women smoking, drinking and chatting with men. She found the whole situation very uncomfortable. I was often away with the team and she lived alone for much of the time. We would read the Qur'an together and she reminded me of the advice that we should not go to the places where we cannot control ourselves. I listened to her when she suggested that I should spend less time socialising, but I told her that cricket was my bread and butter and I needed to be a part of the team. Eventually, she told me, 'Enjoy your cricket, but let me go back to be with my family and then come home . . .' I respect her very much for her strength.

The winter of 1994/95 proved to be a low-point of my career. I realised I had been lazy and taking things for granted for a while. I thought I would never be dropped and that I was the only spinner Pakistan would want to use. But you should never think you are special and irreplaceable or God will test you out. I was punished for taking things too easy. No one is bigger than the game and if you forget where you came from, you will never get the right direction. There is no doubt about it; I had forgotten my roots and how much my family needed me to work hard. So I trained really hard, took care of my lifestyle and improved my fitness levels.

When I arrived in Somerset for the 1995 season, they were amazed at how much weight I had lost. I was hungry to play cricket again. I wanted to prove that I was still capable of enjoying a long career with Somerset and that Pakistan should think about selecting me again. My hard work paid off, as I took 95 wickets to finish second in the county standings behind India's Anil Kumble. The only disappointing time of the season was when we played Middlesex in our final game. I needed five wickets for a hundred for the season and was feeling good, as the Taunton pitch was dry and turning. On the day of the game I turned up and the first session was rained off. At lunch I suddenly felt ill. I was cold and shivering and the guys gave me three coats to wear. The coach fetched our doctor, who said I had a fever and would have to miss the rest of the game.

I went home to go to bed feeling very disappointed. Although I did not tell anyone, my dream was to get 100 County Championship wickets to match the achievement of my best friend Waqar Younis, who had achieved it with Surrey. Play actually started after tea and I was not in the line-up. It was the strangest thing, because by 5 o'clock that afternoon I was totally well. However, there was good news around the corner: Somerset offered me a retainer for

1996, as I was likely to be touring England with Pakistan, and a new two-year deal, so I felt I was back on the right track.

When I look back to 1995, I know that I was not on the right track at all because I was still living outside the values of my faith. I was busy buying designer clothes and living up to an image that really was not honest to my family background and culture.

The summer of 1996 was spent touring with Pakistan, and I decided to bring my younger brother, my wife and our baby son, Bazal, to England for the 1997 season. I was hoping that my wife would be happier with the company when I was away from home. My problem was that after matches in Taunton I would go home for a meal and then go out again. My wife would often tell me that I did not have to go out if I did not want to, but I would insist that I needed to socialise to help team spirit. This was just an excuse that I made up to justify living a selfish life. My life had no meaning at this time. I was just doing what I wanted to do and not what my family needed me to do. Cricket is my passion, but by the middle of the season I was not enjoying playing. I was hoping for rain sometimes just so that I did not have to play. Despite this, I was named one of *Wisden's* Cricketers of the Year, 1997. It was an honour and I am still proud to have received the award, but my heart was empty.

My selfishness also affected my family life in Pakistan. When I first began to play cricket I would spend time with my parents, brothers and sisters looking after the young ones, playing with them and discussing family issues. When I returned home after living alone in Somerset I would make excuses to sleep or do my own thing rather than join in. I had forgotten the need to make sacrifices for others and convinced myself that I had to look after myself and that this was the right thing to do.

The 1998 season began in exactly the same way. I was desperately unhappy, although I could not tell anybody. I even tried throwing the ball up in the air a few times to let it drop on to my spinning finger so I could get an injury. Despite the fact that I was living a bad life, missing so many prayers and making myself unhappy, I still read the Qur'an each morning and I think this was my saviour. For a number of weeks I would pray to Allah before I went to bed, 'Please show me the right direction. I am empty inside. My soul needs some peace.' I was so inconsistent in the way I lived, but the county treated me very well. This may have been because I never told anyone how I was feeling and I tried to be professional at all times. If they wanted me to bowl all day or coach a group of youngsters I would always do it. In return, Peter Anderson ('Chief') was a gentleman. My wife and I were expecting a baby in July 1998 and he let me return to Pakistan twice to be with my wife for the birth. We already had a two-year old son, Bazal, and I felt that I should be at home when our second child was born. I returned, expecting the birth, but on the first two occasions I had to come back after a couple of days. Then on the third occasion our daughter, Nawal, was born.

When I returned to Somerset I played a few games and we then went to Lord's. I have a good friend, Abdul, in London and met up with him. I told him that I was not enjoying my cricket. He said, 'You have to remember that this is your living. Speak to yourself, talk yourself round and get on with it.' I told him, 'Abdul, I'm a dead man inside. I cannot change my routines. I'm not inspired. I cannot enjoy taking wickets and I do not feel great when we win or when I get money. If I cannot feel anything, what does it all mean?' After a while he said, 'Think carefully about all this. If you don't find the answer, go home.'

Dermot Reeve took over as coach in 1997 and he brought some new ideas about the way we should eat, train and play cricket. I did not accept his ideas. It may be that I was not ready for the changes, or perhaps that I did not appreciate the way that he introduced them, but I was not right in myself, and it was easy to make excuses for my performances by blaming the coach. I told Chief that Dermot was not treating me well and asked him to do something about it. On two occasions he brought the two of us together and said, 'I'm leaving you to talk. Please sort it out between you.' Dermot told me both times that he had no problems with me, but I was feeling uncomfortable about him at the time. I told him that I was not happy with the way he was treating me. I reminded him that after he returned from a first team game he asked a second team player how his injury was. This was in front of me, but he did not ask me about the knee problem that had kept me out of the match. I told him, 'As the overseas player, I feel hurt. Am I that unimportant to you?' He tried to assure me that he did not mean to hurt my feelings or ignore me, but I was not convinced.

Looking back, I can see that I was not always interpreting Dermot's behaviour correctly. He always tried to keep the atmosphere light and make jokes and sometimes he would appear to put me down in team meetings. When I stood up to make a point he would say something like, 'Can you understand his English?' to my team-mates. At the time I saw it as an insult. To be honest, some of my team-mates wound me up, telling me that he was out of order. I had been influenced by materialistic culture and saw his behaviour as a challenge to my now inflated ego. These days I would not have any problems with the way Dermot acted. It may not be the best way for a coach to conduct a serious team meeting, but I would handle the situation more professionally as a player. The Prophet Muhammad, peace be upon him, said, 'When you make someone a leader you have to obey his orders, because by doing this you are obeying God's orders. Your leader must be respected, even if he makes the wrong decision.' If you talk behind people's backs, you are making excuses. If you make excuses you will not win things. In telephone conversations with my wife she told me to come home. Her view was that Allah would look after us and I needed to get away from England for a while.

I went to Chief for a third time and told him that I wanted to go home. I asked him to forgive me and explained that I did not want any money, as I was very happy with the way that he had always dealt with me. I said that I had tried my level best to stay as long as I could and that he had been a friend to me rather than just a Chief Executive. I described myself as an empty man and told him that I could not help myself or Somerset and I had to leave. He agreed, and I returned to Pakistan as soon as possible.

I cannot think of a worse way to leave Taunton. The county has a long history and many great players have represented Somerset over the years. Men such as Viv Richards, Sunil Gavaskar, Joel Garner and Ian Botham were highly respected and I believe that I received similar respect when I was there. Playing county cricket had helped me to move from thinking that I was a back-up bowler to Wasim and Waqar to believing that I was a match-winner. For this I will always be grateful.

When I had first arrived at Somerset I would speak to everyone around me and on occasions make tea for the catering staff. I believe it is hugely important to say 'Good morning!' first to doormen, ground staff or anyone else, because as the Prophet Muhammad, peace be upon him, says, 'If you make the effort to go towards people, you will become a better person yourself.' In Western society I see people in a bad mood who do not even say 'Good morning' to their family and friends. I see 'superstars' who lack the humility to greet the doorman when they get to the ground. I had become that kind of person, and I knew that I had to go home to my wife and family.

16

Finding the Way

'Inshalla'

I first met my wife in 1989 as I was starting to play for Pakistan. I was in the squad but did not play many matches because Abdul Qadir was playing at that time. My wife was fifteen when she and her family came to the International Hotel in Lahore for dinner. I was also eating in the restaurant with the rest of the squad. Her brother recognised us, and although she had no idea about cricket she was sent to our table for the autographs of Waqar Younis and some of the other famous players. She did not ask me for my autograph and I said, 'Hey, don't you want my autograph? I'm a player too!' So she apologised and asked for my autograph and she still has it to this day. I really liked her from that moment and I spoke to her brother and offered tickets if he (she!) ever wanted to come to a match. He had to give me a phone number so I could contact him, and I used it the next day to telephone her home. She answered the phone and, after telling me that her brother was out, I persuaded her to stay on the line and talk to me. She was nervous at first, saying that she did not know me, but I reassured her and made a few jokes and we soon realised that we really liked each other.

I met her as often as I could when she came to matches with her brother and we would all go for tea or coffee after the match. She was at college and studied hard, so I had few opportunities to see her, but we became very fond of each other. All of our meetings had to be chaperoned, but we spoke a lot on the phone. I remember when we were on a one-month training camp in Lahore and I was sharing a room with Waqar and Aaqib. I would wait until her parents had gone to bed and then telephone her. Waqar would complain if I kept him awake, so I used to climb under the bedclothes and talk to her quietly all night. Sometimes I would hear the call to the first prayer from the nearest mosque while I was talking to her. My hotel phone bills were huge whenever I was on tour, but I did not care about the money because I was falling in love with her.

When we decided that we would like to get engaged, I had to approach my parents and ask for their help. In my family, parents arranged all marriages, often before the couple had even met. Thankfully, my parents were broadminded and they agreed to go and speak to her parents. Her parents also understood that we were serious about each other and they agreed. In 1992 we were engaged and we married in 1994. She is the perfect wife because she does not know anything about cricket. She does not ask me why I did not do well and she does not talk to me about cricket when I am successful. However, she does know when I am not happy with my game and she tells me, 'Don't worry. Whatever happens you will still have me, and we will be together in good times and bad.'

It was to my wife I returned in 1998. I felt very guilty about walking away from Somerset; I knew that Peter Anderson must have been angry with me, although he had the dignity not to show it. For a couple of weeks I was deeply upset with myself for destroying the good relationship I had built up in Somerset. I was not involved in the Pakistan cricket scene for a while and I stayed at home with my family. My wife, who is my greatest supporter, said, 'Don't worry about it. The way you were playing wasn't helping them so it is better that you are here. You have hurt them and yourself and it will feel bad for a while, but time is the biggest healer and you need to find peace.' So I spent time with her and continued to pray, from my heart, each night for guidance.

After I had been at home for a week, my housekeeper came to tell me that Zulqarnain was at the door. Zulqarnain had been the Pakistan wicketkeeper and he and I had shared a dressing-room a couple of times. I knew that he was a very religious man and I said, 'Tell him I'm not in.' When he received the message, Zulqarnain replied, 'OK. Let him know I was here. I'll see him when I come back in a couple of days.' When he came the second time I again pretended not to be in, but as he left I began to feel very guilty. I thought, 'How would I feel if I received this treatment from someone, especially as he can see my car in the drive? I would not want to see him again, but he has said he will come back.'

When he came a third time, I invited him in and we talked in our drawing room. He wore religious clothing, including a cap, and had a full beard. First of all he asked me how I was and how I was getting on with my cricket. Then he asked, 'Are you praying five times a day?' I could not lie to him, so I told him that I read the Qur'an every morning and that I was praying every now and then. He began telling me about Allah and the life of the Prophet Muhammad, peace be upon him. As he talked to me, my whole body and mind felt peaceful for the first time since 1993. Just listening to him had a profound effect. I could not even blink. I had a few questions to ask him, but I could not bring myself to interrupt. He asked me what I was doing for Allah and how long I expected to play cricket. He told me that I would have to meet Allah on the Day of Judgement and that we are here to prepare for that day. He explained what the Prophet Muhammad told us about why he was the messenger and what was important about his message.

Zulqarnain had been a famous cricketer, but he told me that he was much happier living a religious life and going unrecognised. Finally he asked me, 'What do you think Allah will ask you when you die and go to meet him? Will he ask how many wickets you took? Or will he say, "I gave you life, what have you done for me in return? Did you obey my orders? Have you prayed five times a day? Did you plan for the Day of Judgement, or did you think that you would live forever? Did you check on your neighbours to see if they had enough to eat?"'

I knew that I had become selfish. I knew that I had not asked my neighbours how they were. I had not asked if my children were disturbing them. I felt so guilty and began to think of all the wrong things I was doing. For instance, I had told my son that lying was the worst thing you can do in Islam. The next day the phone rang and I thought it might be someone I did not want to speak to. I asked my son, 'Answer the phone, and if it is that uncle wanting to speak to me, tell him I'm not in.' Well, of course my son said, 'Father, you said not to lie, but you want me to tell this man something that is not true.' I was saying one thing and doing another in many areas of my life, and when Zulqarnain had finished I asked him what I should do. I told him that I felt too guilty to ask Allah to forgive me.

Zulqarnain kept very calm and told me a story about the time Muhammad, peace be upon him, was visited by a man who told him that he was making the same mistakes and asking Allah for forgiveness every day. He was worried because he was getting tired of asking for forgiveness. The Prophet told the man, 'No matter how tired you get asking for forgiveness, you must remember that Allah will never be too tired to forgive you. Allah loves people who make mistakes and ask for forgiveness. He knows we are only human and he loves to forgive us when we ask.' Zulqarnain asked me, 'Do you know who are the strongest people? It isn't those who seek revenge. It is the people who can forgive when others steal from them, or hurt them.'

At that moment, I felt incredibly powerful. Inside I cried out, 'YES!' I knew that I was not far away from forgiveness and that I had the answers to my problems. I also knew that the visits of this special man to my house were no accident. He was an answer to my prayers, so I felt I should put myself in his hands.

The first thing I had to do was go with Zulqarnain to the mosque to spend three days with the Jimad, which is a Muslim support group. Part of the programme included preaching to people in the streets and encouraging them to go to the mosque, and I initially felt that I wanted to be part of that. He left, saying that he would return for me on Friday, and I told my wife that I was going to go with him. She was a little concerned and said, 'Why do you need to go there? You can pray here at home, read the Qur'an and go to the mosque to worship.' She had always offered me good advice and I did begin to wonder if I was doing the right thing, because we had never really thought about these matters so deeply. So, when he arrived at my house on Friday, I told another lie and said that I had a stomach upset and was not well enough to go with him. Zulqarnain simply said, 'Allah says that when you are ill you do not have go anywhere to worship him. Instead, stay in your house, say your prayers and get well.' When he said that I felt even more guilty, thinking how merciful Allah was and realising that I had lied to him again. Still, I had lied and I could not change my mind then because my ego told me that I would look really stupid. Zulqarnain left, telling me that he would be back the next Friday.

My inner voice kept talking to me, saying, 'Why do you have to go with him? There is no hot water for a shower at the mosque. You will have to sleep on the carpet crammed together with lots of other people. Why should you get up at 4 o'clock every morning? What will people think when they see Mushtaq Ahmed going around the streets asking people to go to the mosque and listen to what Allah has to say?' My ego was hurting me again, but the following Friday I took my sleeping bag and went with Zulqarnain. I have to say that I did not go with passion, but during my prayers that week I had developed a commitment because I did not want to let Zulqarnain down.

There were a number of us at the mosque, including famous wrestlers, weightlifters and hockey players. On the first day they would not let me do anything. They took my sleeping bag to the room where we would all sleep and I did the first prayer and then listened to everything that was being said. After a while we went out into the street, and I watched and listened as they went from door to door, giving the message of Islam. One educated guy came to his door and said, 'What do you want me to do? I pray five times a day and do all the right things. Do you really have to give this message to me?' He made the mistake that so many other people make throughout the world. He thought he knew everything and could not learn from anyone else.

I think that you should show respect to people who want to tell you things, even if you already know them, because in this way you help the message-giver as well as yourself. This man was quite aggressive and he saw me standing behind the group. I think he recognised me and I felt that I had to say something. I was really pumped up and wanted to say, 'These people are not begging. They don't want your food or charity. They want to give you the message about our creator and what he has to say. If you want to come to the mosque and listen, please join us. If you don't, then please tell them politely that you are busy or something, but don't insult them. They are innocent, peaceful people.'

As I went to speak, Zulqarnain took my arm and said, 'When preaching, the first thing you have to learn is to be calm and pleasant to aggressive people. After the third prayer today, we are going to prepare a gift for this man. This is how you change people's hearts. We will come back and see him, not for our sake, or his, but for the sake of Allah. When we return with a gift he may love us. Whatever happens, you must not hate any human being. You may hate his actions, but you must never hate a fellow human of any faith or none.'

By the end of the first day, I felt like a newborn baby. I felt like I had never made any mistakes in my life and was completely free from guilt. Over 500 people used the mosque, and it had only three toilets and no hot water, so you can imagine how uncomfortable it was, but I was totally absorbed by the readings from the Qur'an. They were read in Arabic and then translated into Urdu so I could understand what Allah was saying about his creation and the reasons for my life. At the end of the evening I knew that, just as my body needed food and water to live, my soul needed to worship Allah for its nourishment.

Zulqarnain came to me with my sleeping bag and told me that he would wake me at 3 o'clock. This is an hour and a half before everyone else prays so we know Allah will be listening. I said my prayer in Arabic, thanking Allah for the day and asking Him to look after me as I was going to be helpless as I slept, and then fell into a deep sleep amongst the dozens of snoring, snuffling and all-night worshipping men around me.

It was the deepest and most effective sleep I can remember. For seven years I had enjoyed money, fame and having TV cameras around me, but after that night on a dusty carpet I felt more awake than ever before. I washed in cold water and prayed in a dark corner. I raised my hand and looked to the sky and cried. I said, 'Whatever happens, I cannot hide from you. Please forgive me. I pray from my heart and I ask you to look after my family and children. I know that

I can only do my best and that everything is in your hands.' I thought back to the times when we would sit around with friends, discussing how much we had in the bank and which car they were planning to buy. I remembered the times we would leave someone's house at 3 o'clock in the morning with our children and drive home, talking about how we would get a plasma TV, expensive curtains or a Mercedes car. When we talked, it was always about getting a new contract or playing some extra matches, rather than what was really important for our family.

At 3 o'clock in the morning I asked Allah 'How am I going to tell my wife and children to change their life? I have made them used to living the life that I wanted to live. My wife had never liked going out until the early hours, but I have influenced her. My son is almost six years old – how will he listen and understand this? He sees his father on the TV talking about materialistic things. How will I get him to go to the mosque with me? My daughter had seen her mother standing in front of a mirror, rather than praying. What kind of a role model had I created?'

The next day followed the same routine. We visited the angry man again and Zulqarnain took him some food that had been made in the mosque. Although we all ate in the mosque – four men sharing a plate and eating with their bare hands – the man was told that he did not have to come to the mosque to eat. When he took the food, he was calm and at the fourth prayer that evening I saw him at the mosque. He was still proud, but he had made the journey.

By the end of the third day I was hoping that my time could be extended, as I was feeling so good. The 'angry' man was also feeling good, because he came for the whole day and went out with the team on the streets. He told us that he never forgave people who angered him, but when we brought him the food he felt his heart open because he realised that we still loved him even after he had been aggressive with us. I thought, 'Wow, this is a great tactic. What a brilliant way to get revenge – change people!' I decided that when I am sharing a changing room with someone who does not like me and I do not like him, I will buy him a gift and change his life. You cannot keep negative feelings for five or six years in a team because you will become empty men. Now I have an answer to such problems. If someone says something bad about you, say something good about him.

I went home after three days a totally changed man. Whilst driving back to my house I saw a big stone in the road and I thought, 'Lots of people cycle along here. Should they hit the stone, they will be hurt. If I move it out of the road, Allah will be happy with me.' So I stopped the car and moved the stone. I felt elated. For the first time I offered old people lifts in my car. Sometimes they were not going in my direction, but I would take them where they wanted to go and then drive on to my destination. I felt great the whole time.

My wife greeted me when I returned home and saw I was wearing a cap. To wear a cap is to show respect to Allah, especially when praying. It is part of 'Sunnah', the way in which the Prophet Muhammad lived his life and the direction we must follow (this includes growing a beard, because the last Prophet wore a beard). She asked me how the three days had been. I said, 'I cannot express how good it was. Allah has given us the finest house with soft beds and many luxuries. We have people to clean it and look after us. We have air conditioning, but I slept better on the dusty carpet under a noisy fan than I have ever slept before.' Zulqarnain had told me that when I went home I had to act normally and not put any pressure on my wife and children to change. He had seen people try to change their families in one day by telling them what to do, but this did not work. He told me to follow the Prophet Muhammad, peace be upon him, who showed his family how to live by example and allowed them to copy him when they saw that it was right.

I settled in and suggested that we all eat together with the children, which we did not normally do. My wife thought this was a good idea. Once we sat down, I asked if the servants had food for themselves and my wife confirmed that, as usual, they had. I then suggested they eat at the same time as us, rather than afterwards. She agreed, and they had their meal in the kitchen. This of course meant that they were not available to wait on our table, so I went into the kitchen for a glass of water – something I had never done before! At the same time I filled a jug and poured each servant a glass of water.

My wife said, 'Are you mad? What has happened to you? You would never do that before.' I told her, 'They have been working hard all day, so this is my time to do something for them. I think this is the way it should be.'

The Prophet Muhammad, peace be upon him, said that when you have nothing to give to other people you should share your food with your wife. This will please Allah and make your wife's love for you grow. My wife was very shy when I asked if I could feed her something from my hand – 'Why, would you do this? You've never done it before!' I pleaded and she allowed me to share my food with her. She never gave a sign to me that it had affected her, but I could see that she became more active and alive with the kids after that. She was flying like a bird for the whole day, because that one incident had shown her that I loved her far more than all the material things I had provided in the past.

One morning I got up at 4 o'clock to go to the mosque. When I opened the door it was pouring with rain. The garage was leaking and the car was surrounded by water. My wife woke as well and asked where I was going. When I told her she said, 'Pray here. You don't have to go out in the rain.' I told her, 'No. Allah will be very happy with me if I sacrifice my sleep and struggle through the rain to worship him for giving me life.' On the way to the mosque I saw a number of people in the rain, so I offered them lifts. I did not do this to make myself popular in our community; this would be the wrong reason. I did it to make Allah happy. I knew that when people saw Mushtaq Ahmed, 'national hero', at the mosque at 4 o'clock in the morning, they would know that Allah is far more powerful and important than a cricketer and would want to join me in worship. Our preacher told me I was a good role model and that people were talking about me. He was sure that young people who were spending their time in parks doing little would be inspired to follow me to the mosque. This gives me more pleasure than I can express.

I should really stop telling you about the things I did because it looks like I am trying to show you what a good person I am. This is not the case here. When we do good things, we should do them for the right reasons and not to glorify ourselves. Allah says that if we know good things we should pass them to others, and I am trying to show how society can be improved if people show more love for each other and give thanks to the creator.

In our society, we should always give to others – 2.5 per cent of our income should be given to charity and we should help our relatives who do not have enough money. All of this must be done anonymously, because it is for the glory of Allah and not for egotistical reasons that we do it. For a time after I returned from the Jimad I wanted my wife to embrace my faith as strongly as me; I wanted her to tell her family and to join me in all of my new routines, but she was slow to act. Sometimes I felt really cross with her, but I met often with Zulqarnain, who told me that it would take time and I should just relax and carry on. He reminded me that for the first thirteen of his twenty-three years as a messenger the Prophet Muhammad, peace be upon him, just worked to win people's hearts. He did not start by giving them rules about not drinking, praying five times a day and so on. Within three or four months my son started to ask me what my praying was all about. I told him that I prayed to Allah for our love, for his health, that of his mother, sister and everyone else in the family and for all the good things that Allah has provided for us. He said, 'Can I learn?' Of course I agreed, and he and his sister began to learn some prayers in Arabic. The first was the travelling prayer, which we said before I drove them to school. Later I overheard him talking to my wife. He said, 'Momma, do you want to hear something new that I've learned?'

'What is it?'

'Do you know how to pray when you travel?'

'No.'

So he told her the Arabic prayer. She did not understand the words, but I knew she was happy to hear them.

That night at bedtime, my son and daughter asked me, 'Baba, can you teach us the night prayer?' It took ten minutes, and the next day my son taught my wife the prayer. Slowly, slowly, my wife was getting there, just as Zulqarnain had predicted.

One morning I came home from the mosque and saw my wife praying and reading from the Qur'an. I did not tell her to do it; she had come to it after seeing me transformed by my faith. This is a great example of the way in which people are influenced by their surroundings: if you are surrounded by liars and backbiters, you can become like that; if positive people surround you, you will become positive.

My lifestyle changed completely. The whole family would be in bed by 9.30 each evening and we would always eat and pray together. My wife called me at practice one day to ask where I was; I told her that I was just finishing and getting a shower. She said, 'Please come home soon – our food is ready and the children and I are very hungry.' I was so happy that my family wanted us all to have lunch together. I had not experienced this in seven years of marriage. As I sat down and started to eat, my son said, 'Did you say the prayer? You should do it.' Before eating we should say, 'I'm starting in the name of Allah who gave us this food.' I had not, and I felt so proud that my son had reminded me.

My family had changed, and my parents, brothers and sisters began to show more devotion. When I saw Zulqarnain I told him that I was amazed that one man could make such a huge difference to people's lives. I learned not to judge other people, but by changing myself and my surroundings I had changed the lives of many others. He suggested we should go to the cricket field, where so many people were living modern lives, and give the message to all the cricketers. I had quite a bit of influence in the Pakistan team and the players never said 'no' to me, but I had seen them make excuses not to talk to Zulqarnain when he came to practice wanting to talk to them. I told him, 'They won't want to listen to me.' Zulqarnain suggested we went to see Saeed Anwar at home. I agreed and we paid a visit. His car was outside, but his mother came to the door and told us he was not in. I was very angry because he, Inzi and I were friends and I did not expect this from him. Shortly after my wife called me and said, 'I know you are with Zulqarnain, so please speak quietly. Saeed has just called me to say that he saw you both from his window and he didn't want to see Zulqarnain because he knows he was just preaching.' I saw that Saeed was treating me exactly as I had responded the first time.

The next day we went back and Saeed listened to us, but with criticism, just like the 'angry' man. I said, 'Zulu, brother, he will not listen to us. He is a modern. His room is full of music and he listens to it before he goes to bed.' Zulqarnain told me not to worry and we returned the next day with a gift of food. Saeed was still angry and told us he knew better than us. However, after he had shared the food with us, he listened more carefully to what we had to say.

Following this, Saeed attended the Jimad and changed his life. His faith was strengthened when his only daughter died most unexpectedly at the age of three. He grew a full beard and spent four months preaching in the remote villages of Pakistan. He had been to Michael Jackson and Madonna concerts in America but was now a changed man. Between 1998 and 2000, Inzamam, Shahid Afridi and many other cricketers changed their lives too. When we toured England in 2001 the whole team would spend time visiting mosques, praying together, listening to scholars describing the life of the Prophet Muhammad and giving to charity. Saqlain Mushtaq had married a Pakistani girl from London and they were living a very modern life. One day he had a big argument in the dressing-room with our coach, Javed Miandad, and I had to hold Javed back. Shoaib Ahktar held on to Saqlain to prevent a fight. After this, Saqlain went to the Jimad for three days and afterwards he and his wife both changed. She, like my wife, covered herself so she was not displaying her beauty to other men in public.

Many of the press asked why so many of the Pakistan team had changed, grown beards and so on. They thought we might have done it to try and get a result in matches, but the truth is that the only result that matters is on the Day of Judgement.

My wife and family were with me in England in 2001 when I was dropped from the one-day squad. I did not want to return to Pakistan, so I went to stay with my brother in Manchester, thinking that I might be able to play League Cricket in the area. My friend and agent, Gary Mellor, put me in touch with Northop Hall in Chester and I played for them for a month and a half just to cover the costs of our time in England.

I returned to Pakistan, but could not get near to the national team although I was performing well in domestic cricket. I left United Bank when the team folded because of financial problems and became captain of National Bank. I worked hard to win the people's hearts and achieved success as captain when we won the PCB Patron's Trophy in 2001/02. This was the first time that National Bank had won the title since 1986/87. As the captain I was responsible for almost all selection decisions, but I was really concerned for those who did not play regularly, the 12th, 13th, 14th and 15th men. Although these players were shy of me because I was the senior player, I used to ask them to help me out with bits of advice and so on. This made them feel that they were important members of the squad even though they were not on the field, and it helped to develop a good team spirit.

As the English season approached, my wife gave birth to our third child, Habiba. I now had a son and two daughters and was looking for work. In 2002 I could not get a contract in England. My time at Somerset had ended badly and no first-class teams wanted me. I spoke to Gary, who told me that there was only Grade 2 cricket available if I came to England. Even Premier League cricket was out of the question because the clubs could not afford me. I told him that I needed to get out of the Pakistani system with my family for a while and would take a League contract that would cover our bills. We were not well off financially at the time. We had purchased land five years before and wanted to build a house, but could not afford to do so. My wife and I prayed five times a day and continued to mix with our friends, but although many of them were highly paid and playing for Pakistan we never told anyone and never asked for help in any way.

Eventually I was offered £12,500 to play for the 2002 season. This was not very much in comparison with what you would get in Test and county cricket, but we decided to come and, as Gary said, the county sides might get injuries to overseas players and need to find someone quickly. I sold my car in Pakistan for about £8,000 and gave the money to my architect, telling him, 'This is all the money I have. Can you please start building my house?' He said, 'With that amount we can start, but we won't be able to keep building for long and your house won't be finished.' My wife and I then tried to sell our old house to give the money to the architect. If we had no home when we returned we would rent somewhere. This was the approach I had been taught in childhood by my father. We had no savings. What I earned I spent or gave to family. I knew that if I kept my faith I was secure in the hands of Allah.

Once we were in England we settled in Stoke-on-Trent, where I played for Little Stoke for the season. Every day off was spent trying to earn a little more money. I coached in schools and wrote articles for the local paper, but I always kept my hopes up for a return to top-class cricket. I asked Allah to make me strong and would train every day after coaching with my brother and sister watching me. They used to ask me where I would end up, but I said, 'Watch. Allah will show me the direction.' Nothing happened for four or five months and then, after my family had returned to Pakistan so the children could go back to school, an opportunity arose.

Saqlain Mushtaq went to Morocco with the Pakistan team and Surrey offered me two games. Gary told me that the money they were prepared to pay was not good enough, but I said, 'Gary, money isn't the issue here. I need to play and get back on the circuit.' I played the first game against Sussex. Surrey were going for the title and I have to say that I bowled brilliantly. When I bowl badly I will say so, but in this match I bowled brilliantly! But I did not get a wicket and we lost the game.

I knew that one opportunity had gone, but the second game was still there to play. I was practising slip catching the day before the game and the Surrey coach, Keith Medleycott, hit a ball that struck the nail of my spinning finger. I went back to my hotel and iced it, but thought for a moment that I would not be able to play. However, I was determined and I played through the pain. We beat Leicestershire and I took eight wickets, five and three. As a result Surrey offered me one more game, against Hampshire, the following Sunday. Sky Sports were covering the game for TV and Charles Colville came up to me to offer some work with them. I was doing my stretching when he approached me. Initially I was unsure, and not confident if I was up to the job: I'm not an educated man. I cannot speak in the proper tense all the time and need people to correct me. But the offer sounded superb so I agreed without giving it much thought. Sky Sports were going to cover the World Cup in South Africa where Waqar was to lead Pakistan. They told me that they needed someone from Pakistan to represent the country and asked if I would do it. This only happened because I was asked to play the last two games of the season for Surrey. I only played the third game because I chose to play through my injury against Leicestershire and took eight wickets. In the Qur'an Allah says, 'I will open the door wherever you do not think or expect it to be.' I could not believe that I would be commentating in English for Sky Sports TV and asked myself how this could be happening to little Mushy, although I knew the answer.

The good news continued. Leicestershire contacted us to say that they needed to sign a good seamer and once that was sorted they wanted to sign me as an overseas player for the next season. Shortly after, Gary spoke to Sussex, who said that they were interested in me. Two days later Sussex called me to a meeting with the coach Peter Moores, the chairman and chief executive. I was supposed to go to Leicester where I had performed well, but Sussex, where I did not take a wicket, were interested in me. Allah was opening another door!

Gary had told them that I was a brilliant player and all the usual stuff that your agent should do, but Peter Moores asked me what had happened at Somerset. I said, 'It was all my fault. I wasn't professional.' I did not try to make any excuses and either 'Mooresy' read my body language, or Allah put it in his heart, but he thought, 'This guy's honest and hungry to play cricket.' So they gave me a contract.

17

Sussex

'The club is like a big family.'

When I arrived for the start of the 2003 season I was asked for my motto and my ambition. I gave my motto as 'Inshalla' – with the blessing of Allah, or 'God willing'. My ambition was to win the championship. With the blessing of Allah, Sussex won the County Championship for the very first time in the County's long history, and I was delighted to be able to help by getting 103 wickets.

The local press were very keen to talk to me when I arrived for pre-season, and I tried to help everyone feel confident that I meant what I said when I aimed to win trophies. Sometimes people make the mistake of saying that they want to do something, but don't actually believe it. The biggest factor in Sussex's success was that the coach, Peter Moores, had passion and really believed we could succeed. Chris Adams and the other players welcomed me warmly and it was clear that there was a real family atmosphere at the club. When people were angry with each other it stayed in the dressing-room and never went outside. The following day it would all be over, just like in a family, and we would carry on. The Sussex fans have beautiful hearts and everyone welcomed me. In return I always tried to be polite to them and to all of the people working at the club. During my three years at Hove my wife and family have grown to love Sussex. The children really look forward to coming over during their school holidays and they go to visit many of the tourist sites. Now that I have changed I am happy to spend far more time with my family, and I am sure that this stability has helped my game. My faith helps me keep to a routine when my family return to Pakistan, too. As I pray five times each day I have to discipline my life. I used to visit Portland Street Mosque, but now regularly visit the Dyke Road Mosque in Hove to listen to the preachers and gain inspiration. It gives me great pleasure to visit mosques as I know that my presence can inspire others to follow the teachings of the Prophet. When we play away matches I will go to the local mosques to make a speech and meet people. Many of the Pakistani players also do this.

For the first month we did not play very well. After we lost to Warwickshire, I made my first speech to the team. I told them we should not go into corners and talk about who is to blame. I put my hand up and said, 'I am to blame for this defeat. I will take responsibility. Now, when we win let us all take the glory, and when we lose let's all share the blame. Don't use "him" or "I" anymore. Let's use "we" when we talk about winning or losing.' After that, we started to win games and the team began to believe that we could win matches even when it looked like we might lose. I continue to give full freedom to all of my team-mates to tell me if they see any bad habits developing in my technique or think that I am practising or performing badly. I like to get a pat on the back, but I also appreciate it when I receive constructive criticism.

With only two games to go in 2003 we played Lancashire, knowing that we needed 12 points to win the title. We lost badly. I was on 99 wickets and did not get a single one in that game! By the time of the last game against Leicestershire at Hove, we knew that 8 points would be enough. We bowled them out for 179 and I took four wickets. My hundredth was the last ball before lunch on the first day when I got the Australian, Brad Hodge, with a leg break. It was very important because he had been hitting us all around the ground. I did not miss a game that season, but the number of overs I bowled took their toll on me and I developed a groin injury. For the last few games I was playing through pain, but as I was being chased around the outfield by my team-mates I did not feel a thing. Our innings saw Murray Goodwin hit a record-breaking 335 not out. We declared on 614 for four and bowled them out again for 380 to win by an innings and 55 runs.

...ampionship season in 2003. Sussex skipper Chris Adams is clutching the champagne.

...ring all the headgear I can muster. I do my
...to ignore the pundits who say spinners
...ggle in the cold weather in England.

In reflective mood in this photo,
shot at Hove in 2003; but many of
the happiest moments of my cricketing career have come at Sussex.

Overleaf: Muttiah Muralitharan.
You can see from this photo why
Murali is classed along with us
leggies as a 'wrist' spinner.

Chatting with Warnie, the unofficial President of the Spinners' Club.

Previous: Shane Warne. The most brilliant leg-spinner I have ever seen. On his first tour of England, he asked for my advice. Pretty soon, I was queuing up to ask for his.

The ever-cheerful Murali.

Comparing notes with Saqlain Mushtaq, the pioneer of the doosra. Saqlain is here in the colours of Ireland. This was during a C&G match in 2006.

Behind the scenes at Sussex: congratulatio from physio Stuart Osbourne after the firs innings of the county match against Notts in May 2006. My figures read: 28.5 overs, maidens, 6 wickets, 72 runs.

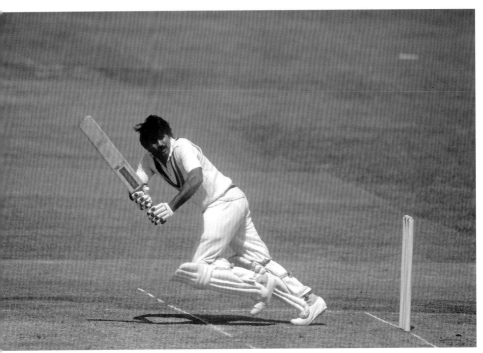

ved Miandad. Big-hearted, fearless and a cricket-obsessive, Javed was a great batsman for
akistan. He battled on through injury during our World-Cup-winning campaign.

he Pakistan squad line up at Lord's in 1996.

PAKISTAN TEAM---LORDS June '96

gland v. Pakistan at
:adingley, 1992.
aham Gooch is
ught by Asif Mujtaba
37 (second innings).

: bowling against
land at the Oval,
lly a happy
:ing ground for
ners, in the 3rd
of 1996.

Arms aloft, I am
overjoyed after
taking my one-
hundredth wicket
of the 2003
English season. I
was the first
bowler for five
years to reach the
landmark.

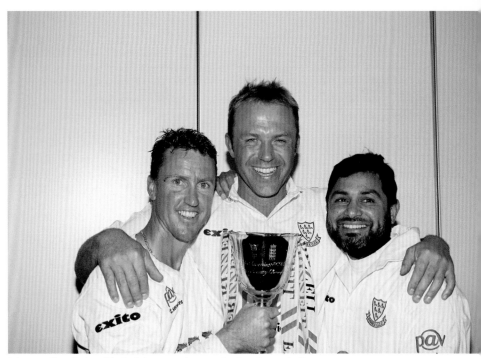

Murray Goodwin, Chris Adams and me enjoying Sussex's first-ever
County Championship victory in 2003.

Victory for Sussex in the
2006 County Championship.
I took 13 wickets in the final
match at Notts, taking my
season's tally to 102, and
finishing with career-best
figures of nine for 48 in the
second innings.
My Championship record for
Sussex:
2003, 103 wkts at 24.65
2004, 82 wkts at 27.14
2005, 80 wkts at 26.73
2006, 102 wkts at 19.91

We celebrated well and I was honoured to receive the Sussex Player of the Year and the Professional Cricketers' Association Player of the Year awards, but I made sure that everyone knew that once I had given 100 per cent, everything else was in the hands of Allah and He was responsible for my success.

In 2004 Sussex had made two new signings, Muhammad Akram and Ian Ward. Both were talented match-winners, but we did not have a very successful season. I think that the expectations might have been too high. Some of us were overconfident, expecting to win because we were the champions rather than through hard effort. The team spirit was still there, and it was only when we looked like being relegated that we really began to play consistently well. I have a strong belief that even if I take five wickets in one day, I must ignore the headlines the next day and start again. This is the only way to stay level-headed and concentrate on putting in the effort needed to be consistent. And if I have a bad day, which will always happen, I have to forget about it and start again, just the same. With Chris Adams, James Kirtley, Matthew Prior and all the other team members, we knew that, man for man, we were as good as anyone else. I led the Championship bowling with 84 wickets and, with the blessing of Allah, I won the club player of the season award again, but as team we could not quite put it all together often enough.

Sussex has been a brilliant club to me. All of the players respect my faith and allow me to pray in the dressing-room when we are at away matches. They will leave or talk quietly so that they do not disturb me. At Hove I can go downstairs, because Peter Moores created a space for me to pray. They provide Halal meat for the Muslims in the team and, when we are in hotels away from home, the boys will wait for me to finish my prayers before going for the evening meal. Some of the players have shown an interest in Islam too. James Kirtley and four or five of the other players have copies of the Qur'an, which they read, and I have spoken to Mark Davis, the off-spinner, about why in Islam it is wrong to take interest from banks. The dressing-room is very relaxed and I remember discussing religion and science with Matt Prior, James Kirtley, Richard Montgomerie and Mark Davis during the C&G match against

Glamorgan even though it was getting tense because we had lost a couple of early wickets. There is a great deal of mutual respect and everyone is happy to listen to each others' viewpoints. Chris Adams knows what my life was like when I was at Somerset, and he has asked me lots of questions about my faith and the reasons I have changed my life.

At the end of the 2005 season I was offered two more years, and this was great reward for another successful season for the team. We ended in second place in the County Championship, and with a little more composure we might have won it. We did win the Totesport League Division Two title. It is very important to make plans for dealing with opponents and we took care of this side of the game very well. We were never complacent and were always looking to improve our play. If I can point to anything that was not quite right, it was that we were a little tense at times. We were winning some games so easily, then lost as a result of this tension. However we acted like champions in 2005 and performed much better than 2004. Every player took responsibility for winning matches and never expected others to win for them; our batsmen all wanted to score 100 runs each game. In the previous year they might have settled for 70. In the same way, the bowlers would take two wickets and then look to take five, rather than being satisfied with what they had achieved.

2006 began very positively for the club and for me. Rana Naved and I took over 30 wickets each before the end of May. I spoke to Peter Moores before he left in 2005 and he set me the challenge of taking more wickets in the first month as I usually start each season slowly. The early season is difficult for spinners because the pitches are damp and the fingers are cold. However, I focused on this target and achieved more than I could have hoped for. Rana Naved is working very hard and the whole team is contributing to each match, rather than relying on one or two players to make the difference. Mark Robinson worked closely with Peter Moores and he has continued to lead the team in the same way. There are no big egos at Hove and he is relaxed and treats us as his equal. He has the ability to make players laugh when they do badly whilst giving them technical advice. Although Mark really knows his stuff, he is also quite happy to ask the senior players for advice. He has made a great start as coach and I am sure he will go on to be very successful.

The talking point at the start of 2006 was the incident with Chris Read of Nottinghamshire. He is a lovely man and a great sportsman and I had never seen him become so aggressive before. I think he was under pressure because the England selectors were at the match and he wanted to impress them with a big innings. The first ball I bowled to him struck him on the pad and we went up for a leg before appeal and the second ball we asked for a bat–pad catch. Both appeals were refused, but the fielders around the bat were very loud and I think this irritated him. He was probably thinking, 'Why are they appealing when I'm obviously not out?' but this is our right and the umpire is there to decide. I got him lbw for a duck with the fifth ball. I went to field near the foot of the dressing-room steps, and after about five minutes he came out of the dressing-rooms and started to argue with me by the boundary rope. He demanded to know why I had appealed so much. All I could do was say, 'Look, if I've hurt you I'm sorry, but it's my right to appeal.' I could see that he was very angry, but my religion tells me that I must not return the anger so I tried to stay calm. I told him, 'If the umpire says "not out" I will have no problem with that. I won't make an issue of it, but I can see that you have an issue with me and I'm sorry.' He told me in no uncertain terms that it was too late to be sorry and he continued to be aggressive. Unfortunately a crowd began to gather and someone shouted 'England reject!' which was really hurtful and not very wise. Then Chris became even angrier and went after the crowd. Chris Adams ran over because he thought that I was getting angry and some of Chris Read's team-mates came down to him. I assured my captain that I was fine and that I understood Chris Read's frustration.

After the game the umpires called us together because they did not want us to hold any grudges against each other. I told them, 'I have no problems with Chris' and he apologised for his behaviour. He said, 'I don't know why I did that, I know I shouldn't have done it. It isn't like me at all.' I ended the meeting by telling him that I considered him a friend and would not expect him to do that again, but if he did it would not affect my feeling towards him. I understand that sportsmen sometimes get angry with each other, but I consider them all to be my brothers and I leave animosity on the pitch. We shook hands and I do not think there will be any more problems.

In both our Championship-winning seasons of 2003 and 2006 everybody participated in the victories. The gatemen, the management, the committee, and players all had a role to play in Sussex's success. Peter Moores and Mark Robinson did great work as coaches. Chris Adams is one of the best captains I have ever played under. He has a good heart and is a very warm man. We should not forget the second team players who also helped to create the winning atmosphere throughout the club. The second team coaches would come and help us and we would assist the second team players whenever we could. The fans at Sussex are superb too and their contribution should be mentioned. I have only experienced enthusiasm and appreciation from the club members at Hove. When you hear them praising you, and not focusing on the odd bad day, it fills you with delight and makes you want to give 100 per cent each day. I see the same faces at matches throughout the country and cannot believe the amount of dedication they show. We played Surrey in a one-day match in May 2006 and the fans filled a corner of the ground and sang 'Sussex by the Sea' throughout. They really inspire the players. Michael Yardy was batting well and the fans sang his name at the top of their voices. You could see his confidence growing as a result. I would like to dedicate this chapter to the fans of Sussex. Thank you all.

18

The Spinners' Club

'People always believe a leggie can win the game. Left-arm and off-spinners can get a breakthrough, but they don't take five or six wickets in a spell; only leg-spinners can do that.'

There is no doubt in my mind that spinners feel part of the same worldwide club and we all have the deepest respect for each other. In Asian culture a younger player will always offer his seat to a senior player. I can give you an example of how spinners treat each other. Sussex played Surrey in a Twenty20 match at Hove. Harbhajan Singh (India) and Azhar Mahmood (Pakistan) were sitting together when I went over to say hello. The first thing Harbhajan did was stand up and offer me his chair. I thanked him and asked him to sit down again, but he stayed on his feet as we talked about cricket, offered each other advice and so on. My family had been at the match and they went home before me. Later, my wife told me that Harbhajan had asked Azhar who the family was that was sitting nearby. When he heard it was mine, he went over to pay his respects to my wife and children. This is deeply touching for me, and such incidents make a huge difference to your life when you are working in such a competitive environment.

I will always have a soft spot for leg-spinners from anywhere in the world. The last time I met Shane Warne was at Hove when Hampshire were the visitors. After the game we had a long chat and he said, 'You're still doing OK and looking good!' I said, 'Thanks, I'm having fun.' We then went on to discuss aspects of each other's bowling and through this showed our respect for each other. In 1995 he had shown me his flipper and I taught him my wrong 'un. I love the banter in cricket, and Shane is great fun to play against. He hit me for a couple of boundaries at Hove, and as he ran to the bowler's end for one of them he said, 'Sorry Mushy, I have to do it. I cannot do it to the seamers,' before running back again. In my innings I hit him to the rope and ran to him and said, 'Sorry, Warney!' He just smiled, and said, 'No problem, carry on.'

We always have fun with each other. In 1999 he hit me for a couple of sixes in the Brisbane Test match and I said, 'What are you doing? What am I doing wrong with you?' He said, 'I don't fancy Waqar so it's your time, Mushy. Wherever you bowl, I'm just going to close my eyes and slog you.'

Muttiah Muralitharan and I are always joking with each other, too. I tease him, saying, 'If you ever come up against me you are going to get hurt.' He replies, 'Mushy, you're the only bowler who scares me!' I'm not sure that he means it though.

Saqlain Mushtaq and I have always helped each other, although he is an off-spinner. In the nets he will tell me if my head is going down, and I can spot when his base is not right and his rhythm is suffering. Anil Kumble will always share a few moments with me. We have discussed how we produced our good performances and offered each other technical advice. I have told him when he is dropping his front arm too quickly.

I think it is fine for players to help each other even though they are opponents. In all sport, teams have to cooperate with each other when competing just to make the game happen. In the same way, a little help can only improve the quality of the game we all love. Waqar Younis is not a spinner, but he is part of the fast bowlers' clique, and I remember him coming into the Sussex dressing-room and teaching James Kirtley how to reverse swing, even though England were about to play Pakistan. I believe that if you do manage to pick my variations in time, or realise that Shane Warne is bowling his 'slider' to you, you still have to deal with it or you'll be out. It does not matter how much information you have; you still have to play each ball, and that takes dedication and practice.

I should say something about Ashley Giles, who has been a very good bowler for England. He took lots of wickets in India and

Pakistan under Nasser Hussain and is a very underrated spinner. The reason he has been criticised unfairly is that people have seen Shane Warne bowling and expected Giles to do the same thing; but Shane Warne is a unique wrist spinner and cannot be compared with a finger spinner such as Giles. Ashley Giles offers a contribution with his fielding and batting, together with his ability to contain batsmen with his bowling. He does not have the variety of Shane Warne, but he will chip in with a couple of wickets and is actually doing a different job to Warney. He should get credit rather than criticism because he has been one of the most consistent players for England over the last few years. When the seamers need a rest, the team needs someone who will bowl 20 overs for 40 runs, and perhaps take a wicket or two. Giles has done this, which I think is why Duncan Fletcher and Michael Vaughan have stuck with him and this has increased his confidence even more. I was really pleased with the recognition he got when England won the Ashes in 2005, but I think it may be because of the good innings he played with the bat rather than an appreciation of the value of his bowling. Ashley Giles has been doing a great job for England, and the thing I like about him is that he knows his limitations and sticks to doing what he does well.

All spinners tend to favour each other because we are all trying to do the same thing on the pitch. Spinners have to adapt to conditions quicker than anyone else if they are to be successful; if you can do that, you have no problems. England used to come to India and Pakistan and worry about the food, the water, the climate and the pitches. Asian people should not think like that when we come to England to play as overseas players; we have to be hungry for the game and work out why we are not taking wickets or playing well, not make excuses about the pitches, the climate or the food. We all have problems to overcome. You know, steak gives me a stomach upset because I'm used to curry!

On a serious note, I think it is vital that spinners stick together and help to develop youngsters into spin bowlers. There are so few good spinners around and in schools I see too many players who only want to be seamers. There are a few good spinners around the county circuit. Gareth Batty (Worcestershire), Min Patel (Kent) and Gary

Keedy (Lancashire) all impressed me in 2005. However, conditions in England favour seamers, and if as a spinner you go for a few runs, the captain will not bowl you again. So, it is hard to stay confident as a young spinner. The captains and coaches of county teams have to trust their spinners, but it takes a few years for spinners to develop their art and teams cannot always wait while this is happening because results are so important. On a flat wicket they will always go for an all-rounder to lengthen the batting, rather than look to bring on a spinner. When a seamer goes for 100 runs off fifteen overs, he will be picked for the next match because the captain believes that he will take wickets. When a spinner goes for the same, he will be dropped; but we can see that spinners do win matches. Look at the Test statistics: Shane Warne and Muttiah Muralitharan have over 600 wickets apiece; Anil Kumble, 400; Harbhajan Singh, 200; Saqlain Mushtaq, 200. With the blessing of Allah I have taken nearly 200 Test wickets and over 1,200 first-class wickets. Spinners can be match-winners, but we need to play regularly.

The ECB could play a role in this by creating an England 'A' team that has to play all the first-class teams during the season. If they pick a spinner who cannot keep a place in a county side and play him every week, it will not matter if he gets hit everywhere because he will learn for the next game. He will not be able to escape by knowing that he will be dropped; he will have to return for the next game with passion, which will make him tougher mentally and, in time, a much better player. My ambition is to open some spin clinics in England to bring on talented players, show that spinners are valued and recruit more members to our club. Sussex would seem to be a good place to start, as I love the area and the people. Ideally, I would live for six months in Pakistan and six months in Sussex.

19

Friends and Foes

'My wife is my best friend. She has always looked after me and she
has made sacrifices for me. This is the root of true friendship.'

One thing I have to declare here is that I try never to make any
enemies. I have been lucky because I have been brought up never to
ask people for favours. When you ask people for favours they can
become your enemy, but when you never ask they will always be
your friend.

I have lots of friends who have supported me from my childhood
to here. My older and younger brothers were my first friends and we
used to play cricket together a lot as children. Bisharat Shafi, the
biscuit factory owner, looked after me and helped me on my way in
cricket, and I will always be grateful to him. When I first played
professionally for United Bank I made a very good friend in Shahid
Butt. He came from a very distinguished family, and was both well
educated and a fine cricketer. He was the man who taught me about
the life of a cricketer. I was not educated and it was Shahid who
helped me to gain confidence and taught me how to be polite and
well mannered when speaking to people. Rashid Gill, the coach, was
a very good friend too.

Lahore is a big city, especially for a village boy, and when I first
went there I was befriended by Nadim Amin, who has since become
my business partner. He helped to sort me out with contacts and
help when I first arrived there and whenever I returned from tours.

When I came to London in 1989, I met Abdul who became a very
good friend. Ours is a 'no interest' relationship. We never look to
gain anything from each other, but will always try to help each other

if needed. My other good friend in England is Gary Mellor, who began as my agent but whom I now count as a firm friend.

My best friends are Inzamam-ul-Haq and Waqar Younis. We started playing cricket together and we have known each other since childhood, growing up in the same district of Pakistan. We enjoyed happy days, bad days and sad days together. I remember when we were about fourteen or fifteen years old Waqar and I heard that there was a first-class cricket trial in Lahore. We could not afford the bus fare but decided to go anyway. We waited at the bus stop with our carrier bags, and as the bus came we ran after it, jumped on the back and then climbed on to the roof. The conductor and all the passengers knew we were up there, but obviously thought that, as it was so cold, if we could manage for a couple of hours we deserved to get a free ride.

The trials were held at the Qadaffi Stadium, Lahore and we were there for two days. We did not know anyone there and could not afford a hotel, so we slept in a mosque. At the trial they did not ask us to bowl, they did not give us a bat and they did not take us into the field. So we went home – laughing! We were not disappointed, and that is what our friendship is all about. Waqar said, 'Mushy, we're not good enough.' I said, 'You're right. From now on we've got to work really hard.' We agreed that we would play club cricket, work hard and see what happened. Some people made jokes about us, asking, 'What happened at the trial?' We never told them that we were not even offered a bowl or a bat. We tried to be positive and told them that the guys in the nets were much better than us, but that we would get there one day.

In our language the word 'friend' has four letters and each one can be used to start a word to describe an aspect of friendship. Inzi, Waqar and I would ask each other, 'Do we have the four qualities? Are we Honest, Loving, Truthful and Loyal?' When we answered 'yes' we were able to say, 'Then we are friends.' Inzamam and Nadim Amin have become family friends. This means that when events happen in our homes or families we advise each other. Sometimes we will act as intermediaries, talking to parents, sisters or brothers on each other's behalf.

Although this chapter is called 'Friends and Foes', the title only comes from the fact that I am going to talk about special players who I have played alongside in my various teams (friends) or who were in the opposition teams (foes). However, I have made some good friends in cricket who are my foes on the field of play. Mohammad Azharuddin, the Indian captain, and Sachin Tendulkar have visited my home and I theirs. I have never been shy to speak to the opposition when playing and enjoy going out to dinner with some of my opponents. I was really pleased to be mentioned by Brian Lara a couple of times when he gave newspaper interviews and we will get together whenever we are playing; and I also spend time with Courtney Walsh when we can. Whenever I faced him he never used to sledge me, or say anything to me. We would have a laugh, but there was no animosity.

I enjoy a good relationship with many English players, such as Marcus Trescothick, Graham Thorpe and Andrew Caddick. I do like to tease players sometimes and Alec Stewart would get a little bit of this treatment. 'I got you five times in three Test matches!' His reply was just as good: 'At what average?'

There is a lot of camaraderie in Test cricket. Ricky Ponting kept dogs in Hobart, where he lived. When I was playing over there he asked me to go to see them race; I was introduced to dog racing by him. I would spend time with Steve and Mark Waugh, so the friendships sometimes go beyond the simple 'How are you doing?' In South Africa when I walked into a stadium I was greeted with a huge shout of 'MUSHY!!!' from Shaun Pollock and some of the players. I would shout back 'JONTY!!' or something similar. This is the kind of thing that often happens when team-mates get together, but I think it is fantastic that opponents feel the same way about each other. Although some players are shy about talking to the opposition, I have always visited their dressing-rooms and offered to help them when they are touring Pakistan. After all, they are in a strange country, and showing them hospitality is the least I can do.

So, here are my two teams of 'friends and 'foes'.

Friends
Marcus Trescothick

When I started to play for Somerset, Marcus was in the second team and he was carrying a bit too much weight. To be honest, I did not think he would make it for England. However, when he did, I thought back to Somerset and asked myself how he had done this. The answer was clear: you do not have to have a wealth of talent to be an achiever. He got there through his dedication. He has a passion for the game and would ask me lots of questions about how I became an international cricketer, how I handled the pressure and the crowds, what was the difference between county and international cricket, and so on. If someone was bowling well he would go and watch them all day. To this day he still does not think he is complete. He takes advice and is a 'learner'. If you watch him in the field he is always busy and learning. He's shining the ball, or talking to Michael Vaughan, his captain, or talking in the slips, or throwing the ball to mid-off. He is doing something all the time and his mind is always on the game. The attention he devotes to these small details helps him. He knows his limitations, but he has a strong belief in his ability and he always plays aggressively in England where openers often find it difficult to get runs.

Saeed Anwar

Saeed is a skinny man, not powerful to look at. He is also the most nervous batsman I have ever seen before going in to bat. However, I have never seen anyone hit sixes like him. He is such a huge natural talent and is a very wristy player. Because of this he was able to step across to an off-side ball and whip it through midwicket. At other times a similar ball would be dispatched through the off side, and if you gave him any width he would lash the ball through point or gully. I think he used to win Man of the Match for Pakistan in every other ODI. People used to say in the dressing-room that if you bat with Saeed Anwar you never feel under pressure. It does not matter how many you score. He has the ability to play against seamers and spinners equally well.

Javed Miandad

Javed was a very brave man who was full of self-belief. If someone in the dressing-room said the pitch was going up and down, he would be the first man shouting to all the batsmen, 'I'll go out there. Let's see how many times they can beat me!' He would not pay attention to the wicket. He said that God gives you eyes and you should watch each ball and play it on merit. If the ball rises high on you, he says you should just leave it and wait for the next one. He really did not think that the state of the wicket was something to worry about. Javed had great passion. He ate, drank and slept cricket and always wanted to be number one. Javed can be summed up by one shot he played against India in the 1986 Australasia Cup in Sharjah. I was watching on TV when he faced the last ball of the match with Pakistan needing 4 to win. He smashed it for six.

Salim Malik

Salim is very talented – I would say a genius. He has great knowledge of the game. He knows the bowlers and where they are bowling and he has all the shots. I have never seen anyone improvise like Salim. He played hundreds of shots from the wrist and was most deceptive. He was a very clever player who scored runs quickly in ones and twos. He kept rotating the strike and often the opposition, and his team-mates in the dressing-room, would not realise how quickly the scoreboard was ticking over. You would sit in the dressing-room when he went in to bat and watch thinking that he was not doing much, but then see that he had reached 30 in no time. I saw him play Shane Warne in Pakistan and I have never seen anyone play the great Australian as well as that. He played the ball so late that Warney would already have his hands up to claim a wicket, only to see Salim strike the ball. He used his pads well when Warne came around the wicket, and when he came over the wicket he played a very late cut with the spin. When Warne tried to use a flipper Salim picked it early and would either cut it or play the same ball through extra cover. Warney had no chance against that kind of batting. Salim has a Test average in the mid 40s but I am sure it should be in the 50s. He is a natural talent.

Inzamam-ul-Haq

God gifted! People have no idea about Inzi. They think he is just a quiet fellow, but he is very brainy and is always thinking deeply about his game plan. The thing I like about him is that he believes he is a match-winner, but he sets himself little goals. When he goes in to bat he will aim to get 10 runs, then 20, then 30. In this way he never thinks he is going to get out and he has achieved superb averages – over 50 in Test matches and around 40 in ODIs. Spinners like bowling against tall players as they find it difficult to get low enough to pull the ball, but Inzi has quick feet and he can play both the pull and the cut to the same ball. He is the kind of player who can destroy a good ball and such players are very rare.

Imran Khan

Everybody knows about Imran. He is a leader and an achiever. It is as simple as that. I am a very lucky person to have played my first Test match under Imran's captaincy because I could see the attitude he has to the game at first hand. He has the charisma that says, 'I am everything,' and that helps the players. I would not say that he was technically great, but he was very brave, and brave people are often technically more sound than they think.

Chris Adams

In county cricket I have seen lots of captains doing different things all the time, constantly experimenting. Chris believes in getting the basics right. He sticks to the old theories and says, 'If you stick to the basics, that's all I want from you.' As a player, despite his eighteen years in county cricket, he still has the hunger and the anger of a young man. I like his enthusiasm and the fact that he will see someone doing well and ask, 'Why is he getting more runs than me?' Then he'll compete to try to be better. He is undoubtedly a great leader who stays calm in all situations and gives you the freedom to play to your own strengths,

Zulqarnain

He is the best man for me. He is a very simple man and very religious now. I played a few exhibition matches with him and saw him keep wicket for Pakistan on TV. I have told how he helped me find my way elsewhere in this book, and it is because of the way that he changed my life that I have selected him for this team.

Wasim Akram

A legend. Steve Waugh said it when he was asked which cricketer he would like to be in another life. He did not hesitate in naming Wasim Akram. Wasim has a great sense of humour and never seems to worry about results. He can win matches single-handedly and will often experiment while searching to improve his performance. He is a natural talent. He is the guy who knows how to play cricket in Pakistan, and he scares all the batsmen with the new ball and the old ball. He can smash any bowler a long way. I was glad to play with him. He is lovely company and a great man.

Abdul Qadir

Abdul was very different to most spin bowlers. He was proud of his art, and he was very aggressive. He was my role model when I started playing for Pakistan and I learned one very important thing from him. He used to act like a fast bowler, not like a spinner. If a fast bowler is hit for six he will bowl a bouncer or something to intimidate the batsman, but the spinner cannot do that. So, if someone hit Abdul for six, he would bring mid-off and mid-on up to tell the batsman, 'Go on, hit me again. You know the last one was a fluke!' People used to love his dancing action and he had great variety. I really admired his enthusiasm and tried to copy every aspect of his actions (he had more than one) and his game.

Waqar Younis

The master of reverse swing. He is incredibly athletic and he has a big heart. I have never seen anyone with as much passion for the game as Waqar. If the opposition need 40 to win with six wickets in hand, he will be the first fellow in the dressing-room to stand up and say, 'We will win the game! I will win this game.' He has the highest level of self-confidence. When everyone else thinks the game is lost, and even when he is going for lots of runs, he will charge in again and again. He never gives up. He is incredibly fast, and it was Waqar who brought reverse swing into the world. I saw him learn to reverse swing and I have never seen anyone master it so quickly. He spent hours experimenting, with purpose, in the nets. He has incredible pace and sprints really quickly, seemingly without any effort.

Andrew Caddick

When I played county cricket with him, he thought that he was the man to bring Somerset success. If you had a problem with your mobile phone, he believed that he was the man who could sort it out. If you had a problem with your barbecue, he was the man who would fix your barbecue. If you had a problem with your TV, he would be the first person to go to your house to sort out your TV. He was everywhere! The one thing I learned from him was self-belief. He showed that whatever you do, you have to do it to the best of your ability. I was determined to compete with Caddick when I first arrived as the overseas player at Somerset. He was so sure that he was the number one player, but I thought, 'No, I'm not going to be second here.' At that young age, I was keen to compete with people and that meant that sometimes we did not see eye to eye, but I respect him a lot. His height enabled him to get lots of bounce, which made him a dangerous bowler wherever he played in the world. On lively wickets he could be lethal.

Foes
Brian Lara

Another legend! I have bowled at him a few times in Test and one-day cricket. He can destroy your good ball at any time. If he thinks that a bowler is getting on top of him and bowling well, he can take away your confidence in a few moments. He can play a cut or a drive to the same length ball from a spinner. He can play fast bowlers from the front foot or the back foot to the same length ball. He has two or three shots that he can play to every ball.

I have a great friendship with Brian. Whenever we went out together and talked about cricket, he would never think that he was that brilliant. If I said, 'Brian, that was a great innings today.' He would just say, 'C'mon, I was lucky.' He was so modest. I remember when he started playing for the West Indies against Pakistan. He dropped a vital catch in the slips on his debut and we did not think that he was that good a batsman. However, Viv Richards was his captain and he said to Imran Khan, 'This guy is going to play a great role in West Indies cricket.' Pakistan saved the match, partly as a result of the dropped catch, but I recall Richards giving Lara a hug as they went into the dressing-room. Now that I know him as a friend, I can say that Viv Richards was absolutely right, but Brian is a good man and never treats himself as if he is a legend.

Graham Thorpe

I have played against Graham many times in Test cricket and know him through Waqar. He has a great sense of humour. He knows his game and knows how to get runs. He selects his shots and then plays in that area for the innings. If he starts to play me with sweeps, he plays only sweeps. He will not try to play me on the up or in the air. If he wants to use his feet, he will use his feet and never play a sweep. So he is a very selective kind of fellow, and it does not matter how many bad words players say to him to irritate him on the field – he will always give you a smile.

Sachin Tendulkar

A natural-born, God-gifted cricketer. His debut was also against Pakistan in Karachi in 1989. He was sixteen and I was one or two years older than him, so as youngsters we used to meet together sometimes. We played in an exhibition charity game before he was due to face Waqar and Wasim. Everyone said that he was going to be a star, but in this game he played Abdul Qadir like a school kid. He took every ball on his pads and impressed no one. The first one-day game in Peshawar was rained off, but we played another charity game in which he hit me for two big 6s and two 4s in one over. Abdul Qadir was bowling from the other end and he went up to Sachin and said, 'Look, Mushy is a young fellow and you can hit him, but let's see if you can hit me.' Tendulkar then hit four 6s and two 4s off the following over from Qadir. Abdul Qadir stood in the middle of the wicket and applauded him, saying that he had never seen a sixteen-year-old hit the ball as well as that.

Mohammad Azharuddin

I loved to watch him play. He was a very wristy player, who could turn the 'fourth stump' ball (the outswinger going away from you that is hard to play on the off side) into the midwicket area. If you bowled on his leg stump he could play you inside out through cover. Wherever you set your field, he found the gaps. One would often think that he was only on 10, but looking at the scoreboard you would see his score at 35 or 40. He was a sneaky kind of player, and a good man to have in your team.

Steve Waugh

I have never seen anyone as gutsy as Steve Waugh. He was the first batsman I have seen who goes and speaks to the fast bowlers as if he is a fast bowler. Ninety per cent of batsmen are very friendly with fast bowlers in the hope that they will be looked after at the crease. If they are hit with a bouncer they will turn away and hope to survive the next one if it comes. When Steve is hit he will ignore the bruise, walk up to the bowler, look him in the eye and say, 'Try it again, boy. You're never going to get me out!' It is amazing that Steve, who cannot pull or play the short ball, has got over 10,000 Test runs – and a lot of bruises!

Aravinda De Silva

When Sri Lanka were struggling in Test cricket, Aravinda de Silva turned up and the level of enthusiasm in Sri Lankan batting improved considerably. Pakistan used to beat Sri Lanka in Pakistan quite comfortably, but then Aravinda arrived and he scored 40s and 60s by hammering Imran Khan and Wasim Akram for fours and sixes. When he did it in the first game we thought it was a fluke, but then he did it again in the second game. After this, we decided that he was a very dangerous player and we needed to get him out. He has since gained the same respect throughout the world. Every time he scored 30 or 40 he would go on to get a hundred. I admire him because he started playing cricket where his only opponents were spinners, but he had to develop his game against genuine fast bowlers. He is a genius.

Muttiah Muralitharan

Murali is really nice fellow. You could hit him for six sixes in one over and he would still laugh and give you a smile. He never panics or sees any problems. I remember when Pakistan toured Sri Lanka in 1994 I had finished with Somerset and he was asking me lots of questions about county cricket in England and was quite keen to be involved. He also never stopped bowling. We played a Test match and he was bowling before the match, at lunchtime, at teatime, during breaks and after the game. He loves bowling. He always, always had a ball in his hand and was spinning it in his fingers and working it all the time. Now, of course, he is a legend. His record of taking six wickets per Test is simply amazing. I think he is so good simply because he spins the ball more than anyone else. Once he had developed his doosra, batsmen had no chance against him. You just cannot play against someone with pace who can spin the ball both ways. If you make one mistake against Murali, you're out.

Steve Fleming

I rate Steve as a captain and as a good guy. He is very modest and has taken New Zealand to the point where they can beat anybody – and this was not always the case. He has had a big influence on New Zealand cricket and I give him credit for that. He is a great leader who took a team with no stars and turned them into a really effective unit. His tactical understanding is really good – he knows when to attack and defend. His bowling attack did not have much variation, but he used his bowlers well in combination with each other. His ability has been proved at Nottinghamshire, whom he led to the 2005 County Championship.

Shane Warne

Shane is a living legend. He is the most intelligent and talented leg-spinner that I have ever seen or am likely to see in my life. He is a proud man and a brilliant guy.

In 1993 he was selected to play in the Ashes in England. The Aussies came to Somerset. I was being rested but was in the dressing-room and Ian Healey came to me and said, 'We have a leg-spinner in our dressing-room. Can you speak to him and give him some tips?' I sat with them and I said, 'On English wickets you must bowl with pace, and you mustn't be shy to bowl with variety. If you can bowl a wrong 'un, bowl it twice in one over to show what you can do.' And I continued with a few more bits of advice based on my experience.

He then played the first and second Test matches and I remember sitting watching on TV and laughing at how brilliant he was. I wondered when I would get to see him again so I could ask *his* advice on how to bowl and get some tips myself. In 1995 we had a long chat and went to the nets a couple of times in Australia. He showed me his varieties. He really knows his basics and I have never seen another spinner who can turn the ball like him. He is also a great reader of batsmen and can analyse them quicker than anyone else. He always believes he can set batsmen up and get them out, but he is never overconfident about his ability. He is the most consistent leg-spinner and he hardly ever bowls a bad ball. I like the guy. He is modest, has a good sense of humour and respects the leg-spinners' art. We must not also forget that he can bat a bit and is a superb slip catcher.

Adam Gilchrist

Adam is the first batsman-wicketkeeper. He sent the message out to the world that you should look for a batsman-wicketkeeper, not a wicketkeeper-batsman. There is a huge difference between the two now. If you are a 50 per cent wicketkeeper, but a 100 per cent batsman, you are likely to be selected for a Test team nowadays. Adam destroys the new bowlers and I have seen him smash Shoaib Akhtar all around the ground. His achievement cannot be under-estimated, because until he came along you would never expect a wicketkeeper to average over 50 in Test matches. He has done this batting anywhere from one to seven in the order. The Australians are so good because they can call on Adam whenever they need a performance. If they need a quick 50 he will deliver. If they want a hundred from a middle-order batsman he will come in at seven and produce the goods. This is not all to do with his technique – it is temperament and Adam knows no fear. His great strength is his ability to put pressure on the opposition, no matter what situation Australia are in.

Alec Stewart

Stewie was a very professional cricketer. I respect him highly for this approach to every aspect of his game, from his fitness and match preparation to the maintenance of his gear. I think he is a superb role model for all youngsters who can learn how to discipline their life from him. He would study the bowlers that he was about to face in a series and practise against the same types so he would be prepared for everything that might happen in the matches. Before facing Wasim Akram he would spend hours in the nets with a left-arm seamer.

Shaun Pollock

Shaun is the first South African of my era who can be considered a genuine all-rounder. He is a sweet timer of the ball who plays like a proper batsman. He is a dangerous player whom we used to be worried about. Donald was a great bowler but the Pakistan team thought Pollock was more dangerous. He hardly gives you runs – much like Glenn McGrath. He was a very talented batsman, too, and we knew that he could win matches for South Africa. It is not easy to be a fast bowler and then come out and bat at number 7 or 8 to score a hundred. He has a special talent, and I consider him to be a great player.

Anil Kumble

I respect him a lot, both as a gentleman and as a leg-spinner. Over the years he has been criticised, even by Indian cricketers, as someone who only performs well in India. The suggestion is that he needs the help of the Indian wickets and gets hammered whenever he goes abroad. I do not believe that. He has taken over 500 Test wickets for his country. When most people are criticised they will try to change their action and be somebody else, but he never did that. He has achieved this for his country by staying true to himself.

Malcolm Marshall

What a genius! He was a brilliant guy and whenever I met him it never felt like my hero was talking to me. He just seemed like a friend. Once the West Indies were playing in Pakistan and Inzamam was playing his first Test against Macko. Inzi was a young fellow, a young blood, and he was not wearing a helmet against Malcolm Marshall. He scored 27 runs, but later Macko came over to me and said, 'Hey, Mushy, man. Is he your friend?' I said, 'Yes.' He said, 'Tell him next time to wear a helmet.' When I asked him why he said, 'Because with his technique, if someone bowls a good bouncer to him and he misses it, that will be it!' I told Inzi afterwards and he said, 'OK' and from then on he wore a helmet.

Macko would always believe that he could get five or six wickets in one spell, even on a wicket that was supposed to be only for spinners. He used to read batsmen brilliantly. You might pull a ball and believe you can do it again, but he would change the pace from, say, 80mph to 87mph the next ball and you would just miss it and – bang! – it would be on your head. He was a dangerous bowler.

Courtney Walsh

A real gentleman in a West Indies team where most players would swear at you and tell you that you could not bat and that they were going to see your blood. Courtney would walk up to the batsman, look at him and then walk back without saying anything. He was the first person to get 500 wickets in Test cricket and this was a great achievement. In the 1987 World Cup in Pakistan we needed about 10 or 12 runs to win from our last wicket. As Courtney Walsh ran in to bowl, Salim Jaffer left his crease at the bowler's end too early trying to look for quick runs. Walsh would have been in his rights to halt his action and run him out; instead he stopped, with Jaffer halfway down the wicket, and teased him by pretending to go for the bails until he regained his ground. Walsh was laughing, but he let Pakistan stay in the match and we won when Abdul Qadir hit him for six. The West Indies could have won the World Cup had he run out Salim Jaffer. After the tournament, the Spirit of Sportsmanship prize was awarded to Walsh and it was well deserved. I always admired him for this. He is a great guy.

Andrew Flintoff

He has proved himself to be an excellent all-rounder and has brought back self-belief to English cricket. He inspires the players around him and the whole nation. He is proud and dangerous. He is a nice fellow who is innocent, almost naïve I think, but he is very talented. It is good to have players in your side who are straightforward. He is a very quick bowler with a lot of patience and discipline. In the field he is an excellent slip catcher. He can bat with great power, but he is not a slogger; he treats every ball on its merits. He has the ability to play a ball from the off side over mid-on, but can also hit some big sixes. Every six is hit cleanly. There is no fluke to it, and he should keep playing the same way and be on his guard when people accuse him of losing his wicket by playing aggressively.

20

Vision

'England is a wonderful place where everyone is free to live their lives as they wish. It has people of all faiths and none living side by side in peace. There are mosques, temples, synagogues and churches and people of all nationalities and colours. It is a fantastic country, but I don't think enough people think hard enough about why they are here and how they should live their lives.'

Cricket, along with the rest of the world, is moving at a frantic pace. I am not keen on some aspects of technology that are used to play back umpiring decisions and analyse them; I do not think this is helpful to the umpire's authority, but I do recognise that TV and technology have played a huge part in making cricket popular. Twenty20 has provided youngsters with role models and the TV coverage is brilliant in encouraging people to watch and identify with players. I never see an empty seat at Twenty20 matches, which is fantastic for the players and the game. When I first came to England we saw kids playing cricket in the streets, but then this stopped as football took over. Now I am seeing it again. The England team's performance in the Ashes has motivated a lot of youngsters to play and they are looking for the thrill of the real game. I saw kids playing in Hove Park with stumps and a hard ball recently, although there was no wicket. I think they have listened to players explaining what they are doing through the radio micro-phones used in Twenty20 and they want to feel the same thing. In Pakistan, cricket was dying. It was a country that was fanatical about cricket, but in the last three or four years you hardly saw any people coming into the grounds for first-class or Test cricket. I think this was because there was no thrill left. The passion had left the people; but now, with Twenty20, it is back.

Fortunately, I was born into a system where I do not get worried if things do not always go my way. I try to stay positive. You must learn to enjoy the bad days as well, when things do not always turn out as you hoped they might; you cannot have all good days.

I have always tried to maintain my discipline because I believe if you are humble and disciplined outside the ground then you will get better results in the ground. I do not understand why people get angry and throw their bat around when they get out. They will not get a chance to replay the innings, so what is the point? If you are a good cricketer, but not a nice human being, then you will have gained no respect when you have folded up your whites. On the other hand, if you behave in a good manner you will get more respect from people, and this will continue when you have finished your career. Some kids get disappointed so quickly if they do well and do not get mentioned, but I was strong enough to cope with the lack of recognition after the Under-19 World Cup. Even at that young age, because of my upbringing I was strong enough to face reality. I realised I had been lucky to get where I was and be well-supported, so I took this little knock-back in my stride.

I think you can learn from every experience. The ancient prophet Ali Hazarat (cousin of the Prophet Muhammad, peace be upon him) said half of your education is completed if you think you do not know anything. Some people think they know everything and they will not ask if they are unsure because they see it is a sign of weakness. If I have a stomachache and I do not go to my physio, how can I get better? I am not a doctor, so I trust someone who is qualified. The bottom line for me is: do not be shy, you will be wise if you ask about something you do not understand, and it may well save embarrassment later on in life.

If I can offer youngsters some advice, I would say always treat success and failure in the same way. I became a different player as Imran helped to boost me up, and I realised there really was no reason to be scared of failure or to run away from the game when things were not going my way. That is why players like Sachin

Tendulkar, Inzamam and Steve Waugh do so well: they do not play with the fear of getting out. I was prepared for the bad days I would inevitably have, and I was determined to be the same person whether I was doing well or not. My first aim was, and is, to be a team man. I give my best whatever happens, but I do not worry if things do not work out. I realise there is always room for improvement. Some days I can bowl well and not get wickets, but on other days I will take wickets when I have not bowled well. That is cricket. However, one thing I always try to do is have fun. I will always give my best, though I try not to take the game too seriously because only God can stop me eating my dinner at the end of a day. If I do not perform well, I should face it instead of making excuses. If I raise my hand and say I was not good enough today then people will respect me for my honesty.

I prefer people to respect me for being a human being first of all and I do not want people respecting me just because I have played well at cricket. If I do well, then I like to share my happiness with the team and spend time with players who are not having such a good time, because I realise it may be me having a bad time the next day. When someone gets five wickets they deserve compliments, but my father said, 'When you are having a good time, do not forget those people who are having a bad time.' If you have that attitude then your team-mates will always wish the best for you. It is easy to be big-headed and forget others who may well have helped you on your way, but why not help them out instead and tell them it could be them tomorrow? People will appreciate it. Do not make excuses or fear the media if they are criticising you. Raise your hand and say, 'Yes, I made a mistake, it was a bad performance.' Do not say, 'the wicket wasn't turning' or 'our fielders didn't perform well.'

I read the Qur'an every day and I realise that humans are the weakest creatures. They forget things very easily. They also have great trouble in being happy with what they have. It is easy to be envious of the person who has a Ferrari, a BMW, a Mercedes, the big five-bedroom house, great lawn and swimming pool. It is so easy to be greedy and materialistic and I have to admit I sometimes start to think like that, but I try to stop myself very quickly. When you think that way, you can never win. The next thing you know, you want a private plane and so on. The process never stops. If you are in the materialistic race, it will take you to the jungle. You cannot find peace and you always want more. Your mind will not rest. If you think like this, you will not enjoy your successes and good times. When you get a lot of runs or wickets you start to ask what you will get for the performance – 'Should I get a bonus or a raise in my contract?' – and that starts to take over your mind so you do not even enjoy your success.

Ask yourself. If you win £7million on the lottery and the next day find you have cancer, which one will you think about?

When I was at Somerset I used to buy designer clothes, but I soon realised that if you have the finest shirt money can buy, someone will criticise you for the colour of your socks. The best shoes in the world will not help you to walk in a straight line or become a better person. Reading the Qur'an every morning brings me down to earth very quickly. I think I am very lucky to be healthy and have perfect children, and when I look at life like that I do not care so much about my bad days at cricket and whether I have got five wickets. Whether you are a good or bad cricketer, everyone is the same underneath! I also think we can learn so much from children. They fight with each other, but they never become long-term enemies and they are always willing to share. I would never tell my kids not to talk to other children because they do not have much. I would rather encourage them to share their pocket money to help them out. But if you want to help someone, I think it is important you do it for the right reasons. If they ask you for a favour, do not wonder if they are bluffing; do it for God who gave you life. If you are giving something to a person for your own interest at a later date then you are doing it as a businessman, not to help that person out.

There will be times when your game gets hammered, you get dropped or are badly injured, but I always try to stay the same guy throughout all these highs and lows. It helps me out a lot in general life. If you do well and the media are showing an interest in you, it is wise to keep your thoughts to yourself. It is not a good idea to tell them how good you are. Now, do not get me wrong: I love doing well, of course, and it is a fantastic feeling; but if, for example, I get wickets and Inzi is not doing well, he does not want to hear me talk about myself because it hurts him if he is having a bad time. You have to be careful and control what you say.

My father used to pray at 4 o'clock in the morning and ask Allah to help me to be a success because I was working so hard. He had a great deal of love for us all. He and my mother gave us lots of attention as children. It is the love and attention of your family that help you to realise your potential. Being positive in the home and encouraging your children to have the right attitude is vital for their personal development and success. The same is true for nations. I wrote earlier about the Australian nation applauding their players for reaching the 1996 World Cup Final and not criticising them for losing to Sri Lanka. This positive approach gives players confidence and helps them to do much better. In Pakistan and in England, the people and the media are quick to criticise; they fill the players' heads with doubt and put pressure on them. Even before the game starts the players think that they are not good, and their body language shows this. Is it any wonder that they often fail to deliver, whereas Australia keep getting better and better? I strongly urge everyone to applaud achievement in their own homes and on the TV and to recognise that winning is not everything. If your children are surrounded by criticism and negativity, they will take that into their lives. During the 2005 Ashes the Australians kept believing that they would win, and when they lost they simply said, 'Next time . . .' This is the positive attitude that will keep them at the top.

My wife has little interest in cricket and she keeps me level-headed when I feel under pressure. She will tell me, 'We will always be together, but you will not always play cricket. So let's talk about other things. There are plenty of other things that are more important.' I often see cricketers' wives, girlfriends and children at matches and I think this is a good thing, although my family rarely comes to the ground to see me play. My marriage is such an important part of my life that I am saddened when I see so many family breakdowns in Europe and America. I do not believe that people have enough commitment to each other in these societies.

My wife has made so many sacrifices for me, and continues to do so, but she is secure knowing that when I finish playing cricket our family will have better facilities than we had as children. My father had the same commitment to my mother and their family and I am just carrying this on.

I make no apologies for my belief that the man should earn the money and the wife should stay at home and look after the children. I cannot see the point of having the money to buy your children material things if you do not spend time with them. If you spend a fortune on computer games, DVDs, clothes and toys, but spend no time with your child, I do not think you have given him or her anything. I know it is very hard in England and other Western countries where you both think that you need to work to pay the mortgage and everything, but I still I believe that if you can eat three meals a day yet cannot afford to buy a car because your wife stays at home, sooner or later you will see that the best things you gave your children were time and love.

To this day I still cannot write a cheque. I do not know how to do it. Although I am the only person earning money in our family I give it all to my wife and she organises our accounts. I know that we need to pay the bills and earn enough money through honest work to look after our family, but I have no interest in material things and leave that to others.

During my first year as a Pakistan player, I did not receive any money. I was so thrilled to be selected that I did not even think to set up a way to transfer the money to my bank account. So, at the end of the year, I received a lump sum of 24,000 rupees, which was a huge amount in those days. When I returned to Sahiwal I took my brother straight to the motorbike shop and bought a brand new Honda C70. This was for my brother and for all of my family to use. It meant that my father could be taken to work and not have to cycle. My mother would not have to walk to the shops and my sister could be taken to school instead of walking so far.

It made me very proud to think that I was able to do this for my family. We had no material possessions in those days; I only had one shalwar kameez (tunic and trousers). However, we would always sit

together for our meals and my brothers and sisters would ask me
'How is United Bank? Did you see Javed Miandad? Did you see
Abdul Qadir? How do they treat you? Did you get any photographs?' I would have to admit that, even though I was playing with
these great players, sharing their dressing-room and hotel and
travelling on the same coach, I was too shy to even sit next to them.
I used to put my cricket bag behind them, never in front, and would
watch them constantly to learn how to behave and to play. They
were my role models and I never thought of myself as their equal.

I still look after my mother and I looked after my father until he
died. How many children now have time to look after their parents?
Old people's homes are full of parents whose children are living in
big houses with big cars. If I was in that situation I would have to
ask, 'What's the point of having these material possessions if I have
lost sight of what is actually important?' I think that Western
societies are creating problems for themselves by not giving enough
time to their children. If my neighbour's children cry, it causes havoc
to me. It is an annoyance. If my children cry, it causes a pain in my
heart because they are my flesh and blood. This love is so important
in looking after children. Nurseries do not have this, so they cannot
look after children as well as parents. My mother slept in the wet
places in our house so her children could sleep in the dry areas. My
father worked really hard to feed us. How could I not think about
that when they needed support in old age? Commitment to your
wife or husband is very important, but you should also keep your
commitment to your parents, brothers and sisters. If you do this,
God will look after you. My wife understands my commitment to
my family, but we are also deeply committed to her family if they
need support. Having lots of money and a big house will not make
you happy if you are the kind of person who puts his father or
mother in an old people's home. Why not? Because your children
will get their lead from you and you know that you will end up in
the same place!

I had always been taught that Allah would take care of you if have
dignity and are not afraid to work for honest money. My family
began to receive his blessings when my father was offered a

percentage of the profits from the cotton factory in addition to his salary. With his extra money and mine, we were able to buy a piece of land and build a bigger house with more rooms so we did not have to share bedrooms any more. My father was so proud because he had been honest all his life, had never taken advantage of anyone else, and could now see that he was reaping his reward from God. I am very grateful to my father for instilling this wisdom in me and providing a firm foundation for my life.

I will never forget my father's advice. He always said: 'Live and enjoy today. Do not save your money for a big house, or material possessions. Do not even think about the future, because Allah will take care of that. Just make sure you are looking after the people around you.' I have built the house, I have worked for Sky Sports, I am still involved in Pakistan cricket and I have a contract with Sussex until 2007. I am obliged to Allah for all the things that have come my way. Cricket is important, but I have to say thank you to Allah for many other things. I have eyes that see and legs that walk. My children are healthy and my life is peaceful. Inshalla.

Appendix

Career Statistics

Test Match summary

	Mat	Runs	HS	BatAv	100	50	W	BB	BowlAv	5w	Ct
overall	52	656	59	11.71	0	2	185	7/56	32.97	10	23
v Australia	9	152	48*	11.69	0	0	35	5/95	42.31	2	4
v England	9	79	20	7.18	0	0	33	6/78	32.90	2	4
v India	1	13	12	6.50	0	0	4	2/64	37.50	0	1
v New Zealand	6	142	42	15.77	0	0	35	7/56	20.05	3	2
v South Africa	8	121	59	20.16	0	1	29	6/78	29.82	1	5
v Sri Lanka	6	34	26	8.50	0	0	17	3/34	40.52	0	3
v West Indies	9	39	12*	6.50	0	0	24	5/35	33.66	2	4
v Zimbabwe	4	76	57	15.20	0	1	8	2/24	39.87	0	0

Test summary
Season by season

Season	M	R	HS	AV	50s	W	BB	Av	5wk	Ct
1989/90	1	4	4	2.00	0	1	1/72	141.00	0	0
1990/91	2	10	5*	10.00	0	3	2/56	33.33	0	0
1992	5	35	11	5.83	0	15	3/32	31.66	0	1
1992/93	2	27	12*	9.00	0	4	3/87	38.25	0	0
1993/94	3	19	18	6.33	0	6	3/79	34.16	0	2
1994	2	5	5*	5.00	0	6	3/34	19.33	0	1
1994/95	3	63	27	15.75	0	9	4/121	46.11	0	1
1995/96	3	39	24	6.50	0	28	7/56	19.82	3	1
1996	3	44	20	11.00	0	17	6/78	26.29	2	3
1996/97	4	109	42	21.80	0	28	6/84	25.07	2	1
1997/98	10	163	59	20.37	2	43	6/78	25.97	3	7
1998/99	4	87	48*	14.50	0	9	2/59	56.88	0	2
1999/00	4	10	4	3.33	0	11	3/91	51.18	0	2
2000	2	2	2	2.00	0	1	1/42	153.00	0	1
2000/01	2	19	19	9.50	0	2	1/32	123.50	0	0
2003/04	2	20	14*	20.00	0	2	1/18	99.50	0	1

One-Day International Summary

Played: 144
Runs: 399 Average: 9.50 Highest: 34 not out
Wickets: 161 Average: 33.30 5+ wicket innings: 1 Best: 5-36

Index